DESIGN FUNDAMENTALS

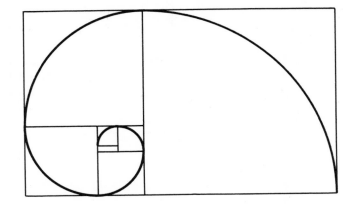

DESIGN FUNDAMENTALS

ROBERT GILLAM SCOTT ASSOCIATE PROFESSOR
DEPARTMENT OF DESIGN, DIVISION OF THE ARTS
YALE UNIVERSITY

McGRAW-HILL BOOK COMPANY, INC.
NEW YORK TORONTO LONDON, 1951

DESIGN FUNDAMENTALS

ISBN 07-055805-1

15161718 HDBP 765

The aid of the Carnegie Research Fund in preparing the manuscript of this book is gratefully acknowledged.

TO MIRIAM

PREFACE

"Design" has tended in recent years to become a word to conjure with. Its prestige has been exploited to sell almost everything from cars to cigarettes. However phoney the copywriter's blurbs may be, the fact that they find a magic appeal in the word design testifies to a significant change in the general connotation of that word.

The time is not so long past when design meant a two-dimensional pattern—such as a wallpaper figure—to almost everyone. True, there were then as now such things as architectural design and bridge design, but when you spoke of design, without qualification, you were most likely thinking of decorative pattern. What we mean by design today still includes such patterns. The magic in the word for contemporary ears certainly lies elsewhere. What has happened so to change its connotation?

I suggest that the answer lies in a shift of grammatical emphasis. The old design was a noun. Our attention was centered on the pattern aspect. Wallpaper could very well stand as a characteristic example. The new design is a verb. It connotes an activity that pervades every phase of contemporary life. You have only to consider the meteoric rise of the new profession of industrial design to be aware of the extent to which we have all become design-conscious.

This shift of emphasis from design, the noun, to design, the verb, has colored our whole way of thinking. It means essentially that we have changed our focus of attention from various specific kinds of designing to the activity itself. Design is now generally recognized for what it is: a fundamental human discipline, one of the basic techniques of our civilization.

This fact has profound implications for education. It means that the old concept of pattern for pattern's sake will no longer do. Even the specific design disciplines implicit in courses such as architecture, ceramics, or painting need to begin at a more basic level. Education must deal with design as a fundamental discipline.

This book is the fruit of one move in that direction. It has grown out of a course in basic design given at Newcomb College of Tulane University. Any attempt to treat the activity of designing at this basic level inevitably meets certain problems and limitations. I have discussed these at length in the introduction and final chapter. I shall not, therefore, repeat that discussion here. A word about the plan of the book, however, will be helpful.

I have used the established facts of perception as an organizing principle. This approach is no more arbitrary than another as a basis for treating the essentially indivisible unity that designing is, and it has the virtue of clarity. The reader should be warned, however, that this very clarity and apparent logical structure can be misleading if he fails to appreciate the interrelations between the concepts with which we shall deal. I have tried to keep these interrelations constantly focused in the discussion.

A second aspect of the organization has to do with the illustrations. Except for the color plates, they are always integrated with the relevant text. The immediate advantage is obvious. But, further, it will be found that the illustrations, taken with the section headings, provide a visual outline of the entire body of material covered. This feature should prove helpful for reference and review.

Finally, the book takes a comprehensive approach to the nature of basic design. It considers the design process both in two- and three-dimensional applications and treats the problems of color and light.

It is impossible to acknowledge all the indebtednesses this book manifests. My reading, study, creative work, teaching experience, and personal contacts of many years have found their way into it in one way and another. The profound influence of two books on the development of my ideas must, however, be acknowledged. John Dewey's *Art as Experience* has been central at the philosophical level, and Gyorgy Kepes' *The Language of Vision* first put me on the track of using the facts of perception as an organizing principle.

My debt to Professor Robert D. Feild of Newcomb College for his unfailing encouragement and perceptive criticism is gratefully acknowledged. The suggestions of Professor Joseph Weitz of the Carnegie Institute of Technology on the psychological data involved were most helpful. I am indebted also for valuable suggestions to Professor Edward Ballard and Professor Gerard Hinrichs of the Tulane Philosophy Department.

To the staffs of the Metropolitan Museum of Art and The Museum of Modern Art I wish to express my gratitude for their sympathetic assistance in collecting illustration material. I wish also to thank the many artists, architects, and designers who have kindly given me permission to use their work.

Finally, without the loyal support, patient criticism, and unending help of my wife in preparing the manuscript, this book could hardly have been written.

ROBERT GILLAM SCOTT

New Orleans, Louisiana
August, 1950

CONTENTS

ix

1 INTRODUCTION: What Design Is

Designing is a basic human act. Whenever we do something for a definite reason, we are designing. That means that almost everything we do has some designing in it—washing dishes, keeping books, or painting pictures.

When I call this book *Design Fundamentals*, though, I am using "design" in a special sense. I mean what we have already said—plus. Some action is not only purposeful, but ends in making something new. It is creative; that adds the plus. So now we have a formal definition: Designing means creative action that fulfills its purpose. But formal definitions are such slippery things. Ours sounds as if it explained something, but actually it only presents us with two problems: (1) How do we know a creative action when we see it; and (2) how can we tell whether it fulfills its purpose or not? We have to understand those two things before we know what designing is.

Of course we do understand them in a way. (I have already said that some designing is involved in most of our actions.) We understand in the same way that Molière's bourgeois gentleman understood speaking prose. We just do it, making our judgments purely by intuition. *And that is a very important fact*. In designing, intellectual understanding will not go far without feeling to back it up. On the other hand, if we are going to get anything out of our study, we must be able to talk about things as well as feel them.

1

CREATING FULFILLS HUMAN NEEDS

All right, then, how *do* we know a creative act when we see it? As I said before, it makes something new. That is part of the answer, but only the surface part. Creating does not exist in a vacuum. It is part of a human pattern, personal and social. Because we need something, we make it—at least, if we are creative, we do. We have only this choice in living. Either we cut down our needs and desires to fit what circumstances offer us or we use all our imagination, knowledge, and skill to create something that answers those needs. We make this choice separately as individuals; we make it together as society. All the things—clothes, houses, cities, highways, tools, machines, and so on—that we use were invented because of some need.

So far, I am making it sound as if we need nothing but material things; that is not so. We want lots of "things" besides: happiness and laughter and affection, for instance. Our needs are emotional and spiritual as well as material. Does creating have anything to do with this kind of need? Suppose we look at one of those useful things we were just talking about, say a Greek vase. We are likely to think of it as something in a museum and to forget that it was ever useful, but it was. Differently shaped vases were designed for uses as far apart as drinking wine and storing funeral ashes. Making and trading pottery was a major Athenian industry, the mainstay of the city's economy. Creating the vases fulfilled two very material kinds of needs. One was utilitarian—the uses the pots were made to serve.

Greek amphora, about 525 B.C. (*Courtesy of the Metropolitan Museum of Art.*)

The other was economic—productive work for many artisans, merchants, and sailors, and goods which could be exchanged all over the Mediterranean world for whatever Athens lacked.

But why were these vases in such demand; why are they still in such demand for our museums? Simply because over and above their usefulness they were, and are, a joy to behold. They told stories with spirit, wit, and elegance; they were unmistakably made with love and satisfaction as well as with clay. They served their socioeconomic function so well only incidentally because they were physically useful. Most of their value came from answering needs that were not material. We do not "use" them any more, but they still answer a need in us, a fundamental human need we share with every soul who ever lived. I would rather not call it the need for beauty, because beauty has become such a dubious word. Let us say it is the need for joy and honesty in our own work and for their expression in the work of others.

Function and Expression

Creating means making something new because of some human need—a personal one or one that has a social origin. In talking about needs, I may have made it sound as if there were a sharp division between those called material and others called not material. What we learned about the Greek vase shows that such a simplification is false. Human needs are always complex. They always have a functional aspect (by *function* I mean the specific use to which a thing is put); and they always have an expressive aspect also. The relative importance of function and expression varies from one need to another.

To take two fairly extreme cases, if you are a nuclear physicist and need an instrument to measure radioactivity, you will probably concentrate on function in designing it; while if you want to paint a picture, you are probably thinking mostly about expression. Yet the picture also has a function. Pictures are one kind of symbolic transformation of experience. If we take care not to push the metaphor too far, we can say they represent a visual language in which we can state truths about our inward and outward experiences of the world that cannot be expressed in words. As such they are a vital means for understanding and giving form to experience, both for the creator and for society. We all recognize that great art embodies some of our profoundest intuitions. What we are saying is, of course, not limited to painting. It holds for all visual arts where expression dominates. Conversely, the scientific instrument also has expression. That is a bold statement at first sight. We can see that it is true, though, if we substitute "meaning in the form" for the word "expression." (That is what *expression* signifies.)

3

Before we discuss this problem, we should go back to the Greek vase for a minute. Its form carried two sorts of meaning. One was the story illustrated in the decoration. Some forms have this kind of meaning; some do not. The picture probably does; the instrument certainly does not. This kind of meaning need not necessarily be a story, but it is likely to be a content that can be fairly well described in words. The other meaning in the form was the expression of creative joy and honesty in the work. This every created form must have: joy because we can create only through loving skill; honesty because the form of anything is inherent in it as the oak is in the acorn. It is the business of creating to discover and express that form. In this sense the instrument, like every created thing, has expression.

THE PROCESS OF DESIGNING

Next, we shall tackle the second problem in our definition of designing: how can we tell whether or not a design fulfills its purpose? We usually have a pretty good idea about this too. Still, important as hunches are, especially about our own work, we need grounds for reasoned judgment. We can get them best by thinking about what happens when we are designing.

Suppose we consider the designing of a chair. First, there must be a reason why we want to design one. We have ideas about the way people's backs should be supported, and think that all existing designs are poor. We want to try out a new way of using plywood or plastic or a new kind of joining. Perhaps we are hired by a manufacturer who wants to bring out a new line of good but inexpensive chairs. I could go on, but you get the idea. No reason, no designing.

First Cause

In the reason, whatever it may be, we recognize our friend, human need. From now on, we shall call it the *first cause*—that without which the designing would not happen. It is the seed, as it were, from which the design grows. When we put it this way, you can see that we cannot expect to understand or judge a design without knowing the first cause. But what if it is not something we can know; what if we have an Indian banner stone whose original use is unknown? We are unable to *judge* it; we can only *value* it. We can say, "I like it," "It is important to me," "I think it is beautiful," and so on. We can go even farther and say that it shows that it was valued by the man who made it. To borrow a distinction from

4

aesthetics, we can always *value* anything to which we respond; we cannot *evaluate* it unless we know the first cause. Or what I should say is that our judgment is valid only to the degree that we do understand the first cause. We *think* we are evaluating things all the time, without the least thought for first causes. That is one reason why we make such poor judgments. Actually we just take our likes and dislikes for granted, and let it go at that.

American Indian banner stone. (*Courtesy of the Museum of the American Indian, Heye Foundation, New York City.*)

Formal Cause

There is, then, a first cause for our chair. We have thought about it a good deal. We know pretty much what we want our design to do. Before we can go any farther, probably before we have gone this far, we have to begin to imagine what the chair is going to be like. It starts to take shape in our mind's eye. We probably take a pad and pencil and doodle to help us think. We see its rough form, have an idea of the materials we are going to use, visualize ways for joining it. This process is the *formal cause*.

It seems quite clear and simple to understand in talking about our chair. Notice, though, that here we are separating the designing from the making. We work out the form of our chair and eventually put it down in some sort of graphic statement, probably a drawing or rendering and a blueprint. Even if we make the chair ourselves, the construction is a second process. Quite possibly someone else makes it. Suppose, though, that designing and making are not separate. There are times when you cannot get a clear and detailed image in your mind's eye of what you want to make. There are times when the only way is to start working directly in materials with nothing but your half-formed notions and feelings to go on. What happens as you work suggests how to proceed. It is a sort of game you play with yourself, in which each move determines the possible next moves. You work along in a state in which conscious direction and intuition are delicately balanced, until you gradually bring out a form you could never have imagined to begin with. The formal cause is still there, although it is something that you partly discover as you go along rather than something thought out beforehand. Each way of working has its strong and weak points. Chartres Cathedral gained unique expressive qualities through being designed more or less as it grew during two centuries. We cannot design the new home of the United Nations that way, using our modern techniques and resources. If you want to be a first-class designer, you should train yourself to work both ways. The values of both experiences are mutually enriching.

5

Material Cause

We are as far along in designing our chair as visualizing its form. But the drawing is not a chair; it just stands for an idea that is really thought of in wood or metal or whatever. No real form can be imagined except in some material, because it cannot exist apart from material. This is the *material cause* of the design.

Materials are rugged individualists. You can get them to do all sorts of things through cooperation, but they *will not be forced*. You have to understand their nature and work with it, not against it. You can see what this implies for the formal cause—no irresponsible flights of fancy. You do make use of fancy, sure enough, but it is always fancy working through a knowledge of materials. You think wood thoughts or metal thoughts or plywood thoughts. The more you know about your materials, the better and more imaginative thoughts you can think. That is real imagination.

So you see how dependent the formal and material causes are on each other. What we want to do (first cause) will suggest certain forms. Those forms will suggest suitable materials. Or perhaps you have some material in mind that you wish to use. The form you imagine will have to be right for the purpose, and it will have to grow out of the possibilities of the material. Form and material always have this interdependence.

Technical Cause

Since part of the nature of materials is the way you can shape them, what we have been saying about materials·holds for techniques, too. This is the *technical cause* of our design.

We have said that materials are rugged individualists; so is every tool and machine you use. Try sawing a board with a chisel and you will see what I mean. What you want to do and the materials you have chosen will suggest suitable tools and techniques. Or the other way around—a technique you wish to use will indicate the proper material. If you want to make a bent-wood chair, for instance, you have to use wood with a suitable grain, such as ash or hickory, or a resin-bonded plywood. The steaming and bending would spoil other materials. Either way, the form is going to be influenced by the tools used in shaping it. It must express the tool and technique as well as the material. Think of the same head modeled in clay and carved in limestone. Suppose it is a portrait. The form will be different in each case. One will be a built-up, modeled form; the other, a carved-out form. If the stone head were carved in granite, it would be different again. All three forms could still be excellent portraits of the same person.*

* See the compositions by Jules Struppeck, p. 155

6

When we design, these four causes are always present in what we do. In fact, what we do is just our solution to the problems they present. So now we can tell whether creating fulfills its purpose or not. The answer depends on the consistency of these causal relationships. If the form created satisfies the first cause, if it is expressed in suitable materials, if the materials are well handled, and finally, if the whole is done with economy and elegance, we can say that it is a design and a good one.

VISUAL ARTS

What I have said so far is true of all designing—of planning a chair, composing a sonata, painting a picture, or writing this book. Our interest, though, centers in the visual arts—arts you can see. What special conditions does that involve? Think of some of the different visual arts—painting, architecture, dress designing, sculpture, typography, movies, illustration, to name a few. Three things strike us when we consider such a list. Arts like painting, typography, and illustrating are physically two-dimensional. Even when they have an illusion of depth, they are physically flat. Architecture, dress design, and sculpture are three-dimensional. So we see that some of our visual arts are two-dimensional, some three-dimensional. The other thing we notice is that the movies, and the like arts of dance, drama, and opera, have a dimension in time as well as dimensions in space. We must deal with three kinds of visual relationships, then: two-dimensional, three-dimensional, and relationships of sequence and duration in time. That is the first special condition of visual designing to keep in mind.

Visual and Structural Relationships

There is a second condition. Visual relationships exist because we see them. If we cannot see relationships, they are not visual. Yet it stands to reason that there must be something behind them that is objective. And so there is—the system of structural relationships that holds the work together. They are quite independent of our seeing them. Consider our chair again. The size, shape, light-reflecting character, the arrangement of the parts and the way we keep them together, make up such a system. This is the material basis of the visual relationships we perceive when we look at the chair.

Both kinds of relationship are essential elements of designing. They present quite different problems, though, when we try to study them. Structural relationships are always specific. The only way to get at them is to study specific designs—to examine a cer-

7

tain leg or a certain joint in a certain chair, for example. Visual relationships, on the other hand, are subjective. They depend on the way our sense perceptions and minds work. We can study them best by studying our reactions. Therefore visual relationships are much more general. However individual we may be, we all react in the same way up to a point. These common reactions are the basis of visual relations. This makes them a lot simpler to treat than the structural ones. The very fact that they are general and more or less universal, in contrast to the wholly concrete and specific character of structural relations, has lent them a false air of superiority. A sad consequence is that the meaning of designing gets restricted to visual relationships. It was not so long ago that to practically everyone "design" meant a two-dimensional pattern like figures on wallpaper. Our whole educational system is still beset with this misconception. That is why I have had to take you all around Robin Hood's barn to explain what the simple word "designing" means. This "aesthetic" attitude we are criticizing reduces design to one part of the formal cause, the visual part. All the rest—first cause, structural relationships, material and technical causes—is left out of the picture. No wonder "designing" became a pleasant pastime for dilettante young ladies and aesthetic young men. I can well remember in art school being shown in all seriousness how to make nice "designs" by putting a piece of mirror cater-corner on a drawing of a butterfly wing. I think the problem was jewelry design!

THE PROBLEM OF THIS BOOK

Enough of such foolishness! The contrast between visual and structural relations does give us a problem. To avoid the same fallacy we have been discussing, we must work with the whole of designing. That is hard to do in a book. One solution would be to follow a few problems through from the first cause to the finished design. (We shall do just this in the final chapter with the problem of designing this book.) The trouble is that this method gives you a few applications of principles, but makes it hard to see the whole picture. You do not see the wood for the trees.

There is another way around the difficulty. It is the one we shall adopt for the body of the book. If you and I work together, by combining our efforts we can study designing as a whole. In the following chapters, I shall take up the most important problems of visual relationship. I shall try to do this in a way that will make it easy to keep structural relations and the rest of the picture in mind. Here is where your cooperation comes in. There is a problem at the end of each chapter. To solve it, you will have to design. The first cause is

8

the experience and understanding you will gain from doing it. The formal cause is the form you imagine and create to solve the problem. The material and technical causes are the materials and techniques you use to do it. While you are practicing designing, you will also be finding out things you need to know about visual organization.

This is really a workbook, you see. It can do the job it sets out to do only if you complete the pattern in the experience of designing. Perhaps some may wish to do no more than read it. If you already have the experience to complement what is offered here, we can still collaborate. If not, I hope the book may be interesting and helpful, but please remember that you are not using it as it is designed to be used.

READING LIST

Anand, Mulk Rāj: *Hindu View of Art*, G. Allen and Unwin Ltd., London, 1933. Introduction by Eric Gill.

Boas, Franz: *Primitive Art*, Harvard University Press, Cambridge, Mass., 1927. Chapter 1.

Gill, Eric: "Work and Culture" (pamphlet), J. Stevens, Newport, R. I., 1938.

Moholy-Nagy, L.: *Vision in Motion*, P. Theobald, Chicago, 1947. Chapter 1.

Mumford, Lewis: *The Condition of Man*, Harcourt, Brace and Company, Inc., New York, 1944. Introduction.

Mumford, Lewis: *Technics and Civilization*, Harcourt, Brace and Company, Inc., New York, 1938. Chapter 7.

Teague, Walter Dorwin: *Design This Day*, Harcourt, Brace and Company, Inc., New York, 1940. Chapters 2, 3, 4, 5. and 6.

2 CONTRAST: Brick and Mortar of Form

We perceive relationships because of the form things have. (We can also reverse that statement. We perceive form because of the relationships in things.) This means that form is dependent on both the thing observed and the observer. Let us start off with this question: "How do we perceive form?" The answer will give us a foundation for answering our main question: "How do we create relationships?" In a word, the answer is: "Through contrast."

CONTRAST

What does this mean? Form perception is the result of differences in the visual field. If the field is the same all over, what we see is fog; that is, no *thing;* just sensation of light in space. It is not a sensation we have very often, but we know this is what happens. The psychologists have experimented with homogeneous sensation to find out.

I once had it happen to me when there was no actual fog. You can verify this experiment for yourselves without a laboratory. I lay on the ground in an open field one clear afternoon looking straight up into cloudless sky. Gradually, I became aware of a curious thing. We usually perceive the sky as a blue "surface" up there somewhere, "that inverted bowl men call the sky." As I looked up, my whole field of vision filled with sky, that "surface" became blurred. It seemed to thicken and then to dissolve until I was enveloped in blue, misty space. Form disappeared, even as rudimentary a form as the

10

apparent "surface" of the sky. (Make a note here that this simplest kind of sensation has two qualities: light and space. It is three-dimensional. That is a fact that we shall come back to later.)

When we perceive form, it means that there must be differences in the field. When there are differences, there must be contrast. That is the basis of form perception. For example, suppose we put a white ball against a white sheet. If we light the ball and the sheet equally from both sides, we can make the ball practically disappear. The contrasts in the field are so slight that our form perception is very weak. Now, we move one light so that it hits the ball but not the sheet. We move the other to hit part of the sheet but not the ball. One side of the ball will be light against a darker ground; the other side will be dark against a lighter ground. There is strong contrast. Result: strong form perception. Or we take a piece of paper. Although it is a homogeneous field in itself, it does not appear foggy because it is part of a larger field with contrasts. If we want to draw a form on the paper, the only way we can do it is to make part of the the paper different from the rest. We might use pencil or wash or colored paper. Until there is contrast, there will be no form.

Our next step is to find out what makes the contrasts in our visual field. What does the pencil do to the paper? This involves us in the qualities of visual sensations.

QUALITIES OF OUR VISUAL SENSATIONS

Physical Basis

It also involves us in the objective nature of what causes our sensations. In seeing, the cause is light. No light, no sensation. It will help us to understand the sensations if we examine the physical dimensions of light first.

There are only two, *amplitude* and *wave length*. Amplitude means the amount of radiant energy. It is the *quantitative* dimension. Wave length is *qualitative*. It determines the kind of radiant energy. One small group of wave lengths between heat and ultraviolet radiation affect the visual receptors to produce the sensation of sight.

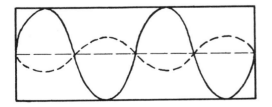

Amplitude.

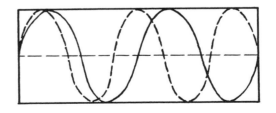

Wave length.

11

Now let us see how these two physical dimensions of light are received in our sense perceptions. We perceive different amplitudes as different *brightnesses* of light. Differences in wave length we perceive as various *hues*. Each hue in the spectrum has a given wave

Brightness and Hue

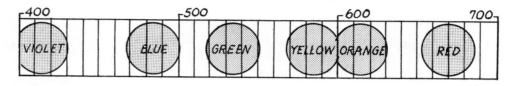
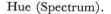

Hue (Spectrum).

length which we can measure with a spectrometer. We see some hues that are not in the spectrum, though. Evidently, we do not receive the program just as it is broadcast, so to speak. To carry the radio metaphor a little farther, our eyes have poor selectivity. They pick up a lot of wave lengths at the same time; only, instead of hopeless static, the result is just as clear a sensation as we get from a single station. This is called *composite stimulation*. Actually, most of our visual sensations are composite. The way color perception works, we can get the whole hue circuit (spectral hues and the red-violets that are not in the spectrum) by mixing red, green, and blue lights in various amounts. Spectrum yellow (wave length 589 millimicrons) and a proper mixture of red and green light will look identical to us. As far as the eye is concerned, they are the same thing.

Composite Stimulation

Composite stimulation is responsible for two other qualities we perceive in light: *achromatic* light and what is called *saturation*. We shall consider these in turn. If all our basic hue sensitivities are stimulated equally, instead of color we see white light, or what we are accustomed to call white light. When we stop to think of it, we mean something quite different from the white of this page. We really mean light that is colorless. The technical name for it is *achromatic* light. We have two distinct classes of visual sensation, then: *chromatic* (that with hue), and *achromatic* (that without).

Achromatic Stimulation

On the other hand, if all our basic hue sensitivities are stimulated, but some more, some less, we have a new kind of sensation. It has both chromatic and achromatic characteristics. This sounds paradoxical, but is perfectly simple in experience. Think of the red from a stop light; then contrast it with the pink light in a window display. The chromatic character of both is red. Something has happened to the redness in the pink light, though. There is not as much of it. The sensation has something in common with achromatic sensation. Another way of describing the pink would be to say it is colorless

Saturation

12

light with a little red added. This quality of the degree of hue purity in the sensation is called *saturation*. The red in the stop light is fully saturated. The pink is considerably desaturated.

We have distinguished four qualities in our perception of light:

1. Whether it is chromatic or achromatic.
2. Brightness, which applies to both.
3. Hue.
4. Saturation.

Hue and saturation apply only to chromatic light. A variation in any one of these qualities or any combination of them will cause contrast in our visual field. Out of these contrasts we build our perception of form.

These differences in our visual field depend on two things: the qualities of the light sources themselves, and the reflecting characteristics of the things in the field. Sometimes we are aware of qualities in the light itself, but most of the time we perceive differences as qualities of things. It is a fact that we see anything only because of the light it reflects. There is a profound psychological difference, though, when we are aware of the thing rather than of the light. So next we have to consider the reflecting characteristics of things. These are of two kinds: tone quality, or pigmentation, and visual texture.

Perception of Reflecting Surfaces

TONE QUALITY

There is the same division of our tonal experience into chromatic and achromatic groups. Everything with hue is chromatic, while all the neutrals, including black and white, are achromatic.

See Plate I, 1 page 87.

VALUE is the name we give to the lightness and darkness of tones. (The corresponding light quality is brightness.) Value really means the amount of light a surface can reflect. White is the top end of this range, black, the bottom. All other tones, chromatic and achromatic, fall somewhere between.

Value

HUE means the difference between blueness and redness and yellowness and so on. When we apply it to the qualities of things, we are again talking about the reflecting character of surfaces. They reflect some wave lengths and absorb others.

Hue

INTENSITY corresponds to saturation. It refers to the purity of hue a surface can reflect. When a red is all red, it is at full intensity. When it has some neutral in it (black, white, or gray), it is *neutralized* or reduced in intensity. The word *chroma* is also used to mean this same quality.

Intensity

13

We can now classify the tonal differences in our visual field. There are two kinds of tone experience: one in which we are conscious of light; the other in which we see the light differences as qualities of objects. In both, we have two groups of tones, chromatic and achromatic. We can diagram this with the corresponding dimensions this way:

	Light	*Tone Qualities in Pigmentation*
ACHROMATIC	Brightness	Value
CHROMATIC	Brightness Hue Saturation	Value Hue Intensity or Chroma

Besides the tonal differences, we listed another set of differences that can serve as the basis of contrast in our visual field. These are the visual textures of things.

VISUAL TEXTURE

Damask: visual texture contrast

We respond not only to the amount and kind of light that surfaces reflect, but also to the way in which they reflect it. We shall call this *visual texture*. It is closely related to the tactile quality of a surface. Some of the words we use to describe characteristic visual textures are taken from our experience of touch—rough – smooth, hard – soft. Others have mostly a visual meaning—dull – shiny; opaque – transparent; metallic; iridescent. We can see how contrast in visual texture helps us to perceive form if we think of a piece of damask. The pattern is entirely dependent on the way the threads are woven. Satin weave, which has a shiny surface, is contrasted with plain weave, which is dull. Through this contrast we see the pattern.

The color white is itself an example of visual texture. If we examine particles of white pigment with a microscope, we see tiny crystals. The white appearance is due to the way in which they disperse the light.

Contrast in any of the tonal or visual texture qualities will give us a visual field that is not all the same. We have found that this is the basic condition for perceiving form. To see how it works, we must study the structure of our visual field.

14

STRUCTURE OF OUR VISUAL FIELD

Light, reflected by the objects in our visual field, falls on our retinas in a pattern of different qualities and quantities. This pattern sets up a corresponding nervous response which is registered as an energy pattern in the brain. Our perception is based on this. It has form because contrast produces structure in the pattern. The parts of low energy or little contrast blend together into what psychologists call *ground*. The parts with higher energy and greater contrast organize together into what is called *figure*. Attention centers on figure, but ground is equally important because both elements are necessary to form perception.

Everything we see that has form is perceived in this kind of relationship. It does not matter whether the objects in the field are two- or three-dimensional, since the structure belongs to the energy pattern in our brains. As these patterns depend on contrast in the field, we can make a direct design application of the idea of figure-ground relationship.

Figure-Ground Relationship

Consider the page you are reading. The parts left plain all have the same tone quality (no contrast); therefore, we perceive them as ground. The ground has size and shape because of the contrast with not-page at the edges. The printing makes a strong tone contrast with the ground, becoming figure. It is what we concentrate on. Each letter, word, or line has form because of its figure relation to the ground.

This is easy to see with a simple pattern like a book page. What about a picture where, perhaps, there is nothing that is merely negative ground? The same thing holds true, but there is a more flexible relationship. The house is ground for the man in front of it. The group of trees is ground for the house. The sky is ground for the trees. Figure-ground contrast is necessary all the way through if we are to see the forms. But, in a complex pattern like this, the same area may have both figure and ground values, depending on our changing center of interest.

These examples are two-dimensional. How about three-dimensional things in space? It is quite apparent that the ground against which we see a statue or building is not part of the design; at least, not in the same sense that the book page or canvas is. It is equally clear, though, that we see their size and shape by the contrast between statue and not-statue, building and not-building. We shall come back to this problem in Chapter 9. For the time being, our focus is on the problems of two-dimensional organization. Let us

15

summarize the important things to remember and to watch for:

1. *Ground is larger than figure and usually simpler.* The last part of this statement is not always true. In many Persian miniatures or Matisse paintings, for instance, the figure parts are much simpler than the highly patterned grounds. They have figure emphasis because their very simplicity makes a strong contrast with the rest of the field.

A. Simple ground.

B. Complex ground. "Interior with Violin Case," by Henri Matisse, detail. (*Courtesy of The Museum of Modern Art, Lillie P. Bliss Collection.*)

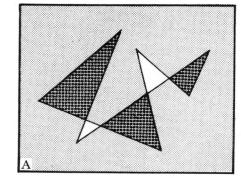

2. *Figure is usually perceived on top of or in front of the ground.* Sometimes, though, it makes holes in it.

A. Figure on top of ground.

B. Figure making hole in ground.

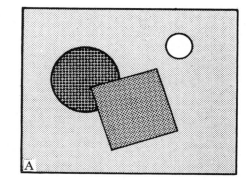
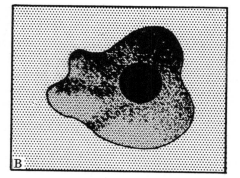

3. *Ground may be perceived as a surface or as space.*

A. Ground perceived as surface.

B. Ground perceived as space.

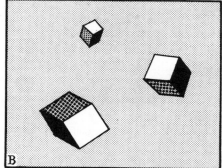

16

4. We naturally think of the form of the figure. *Ground areas have form* too, although it is the negative form of *space left*. Both positive and negative form are important in designing. We should train ourselves to be sensitive to both.

In our examples so far, figure has always been quite different in its visual qualities from ground. That would seem to be necessary to get the contrast on which figure is dependent. One of the most interesting things about figure-ground relationships, though, is the way in which ground can be given figure value.

Ground Becomes Figure

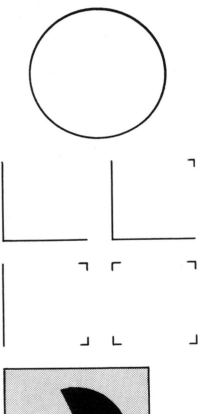

If we draw a circle on a sheet of paper, something odd happens. The paper enclosed in the line is physically the same as the paper outside. Psychologically, it is quite different. We do not see the circular line as something in itself but as the edge of a surface. The enclosed area has become figure! The paper outside seems to continue under it. Line drawing is possible because this sort of thing happens. Lines are really much more abstract than tones, but we can use them to make just as positive an area.

CLOSURE

There is another important fact about the way ground becomes figure. It is not necessary to enclose an area completely to make it into figure. If there is enough indication of *closure* so that the eye can complete it, the same thing will happen. A square makes a good example to demonstrate what I mean. If I draw two adjoining sides of a square, the lines begin to define a space, but not very clearly. Now, if I put an accent where the diagonal corner should be, we see a square. We mentally supply the two missing sides. We can even reduce the indications to four dots where the corners should be and still get a degree of closure.

We can also produce closure by using the edges of tonal areas to define the ground. Whenever sufficiently definite and good shape is given a ground area by closure, it will become part of the figure pattern. This is important in two-dimensional designing, but the corresponding behavior of space in three dimensions is even more significant. We shall come back to this phase of the discussion in Chapter 9.

I want to mention one other variation that is interesting chiefly for the light it throws on figure-ground structure—the fact that we can make reversible figure-ground patterns.

17

When the field is divided about equally between two tones so that both of them make good shapes, we can often see either tone as figure. Depending upon how we look at it, the same tone will be figure *or* ground; and we can make the pattern reverse for us as we watch. This kind of figure-ground relationship can be used effectively in repeat patterns, and occasionally in advertising layout. It is more significant, though, for what it shows about the way our perceptions work.

FORM

We have been talking for some time about *form*. Now we are ready to define what we mean. Up to this point, I have used the word loosely, in two senses. The first refers to the quality of individual-thingness that comes out of the contrasts of visual qualities. It is what distinguishes each thing and its perceptible parts. It is not a simple idea, but consists in a particular relationship between three factors: *shape, size, position*. The second refers to the allover form or composition of the field. We shall look at these ideas in turn.

SHAPE implies some degree of organization in the thing. Unless the shape is recognizable, we call a thing "shapeless." We mean not literally that we can see no shape in it, but that it is not a *good* shape. It is hard to perceive as a definite thing because it is disorganized. I shall use the word "good" in this sense a number of times in discussing form.

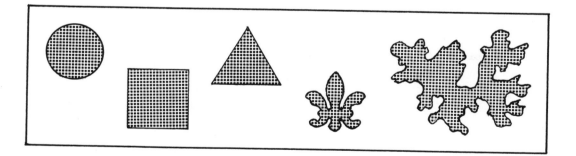

SIZE is always a relative matter. We unconsciously compare everything with our own size; things are small and big in relation to ourselves. But small and big have another meaning, also relative. In a given design, sizes relate to each other. We can have something "big" in a miniature, and the show window in relation to the skyscraper is small.

18

POSITION. Although size, as we have just seen, involves comparisons within the design, both shape and size are properties of all the forms and parts of forms in a pattern. *Position* has to be described on the basis of the whole organization. Position has no meaning except in relation to the field itself. This leads us to the consideration of the second sense of the word "form," that of allover form, or *composition*.

COMPOSITION

I am not too happy with the term "composition," but it is the best one available. ("Compositional form" or "allover form" are too awkward.) The ambiguity comes from the general association of composition with something you do to a painting. It is much more than that. We mean by it the total organization, including figure and ground, of any design. All the individual forms and parts of forms have not only shape and size but their *position* in it.

Thus, the concept of composition begins with the design field. This field provides the limits of a unique universe which you create. Its basic laws are determined by the character of the field. They may be explicit, as when you select a certain format for a picture or page layout. They may be only approximate, as when you decide on the scale of a building or piece of sculpture. In either case, the way you develop your universe will be conditioned by its inherent laws. To give one illustration, a rectangular format with a long vertical dimension has completely different potentialities and limitations from the same format in a horizontal position. The concept is realized in the creation of an organic unity between the field and the forms in it. Through the relationships you establish, the rightness of which is determined by the unique character of the organization itself, a new entity is created. As in a man or a tree, the relationships that make up unity are both structural and visual. Our interest is in the visual side at present. But you see how composition means structural organization, too, and how structural organization underlies the visual relationships.

How to make an organization with this quality of organic unity; that is, how to compose, is the problem we shall be studying from various angles in the remainder of this book.

READING LIST

Koffka, Kurt: *Principles of Gestalt Psychology*, Harcourt, Brace and Company, Inc., New York, 1935. Chapters 4 and 5.

Köhler, Wolfgang: *Gestalt Psychology*, Liveright Publishing Corp., New York, 1947. Chapter 5.

PROBLEM I

Purpose:

1. To help you develop a clear understanding of the chromatic-achromatic, value, hue, and intensity dimensions of color.
2. To study the effect of contrast in these dimensions, and in visual texture upon figure-ground organization.

Problems:

1. Select a suitable format, say half of an 8- by 10-inch sheet of drawing paper for your compositions. Using clipping material, as explained below, make four abstract designs.
   a. One pattern is to be built out of achromatic value contrasts.
   b. One is to be built out of value and intensity contrasts within a scheme of a single hue.
   c. One is to be built primarily out of hue contrasts. (Some value and intensity contrast will be inevitable. Put the emphasis on hue, though.)
   d. One is to be built primarily out of intensity contrasts. (Some value and hue contrast will be inevitable. Put the emphasis on intensity.)
2. Using the same format and clipping material, make a design that depends primarily on visual texture contrast.
3. Using the same format, make a design by texturing the paper itself so that different parts will reflect light differently.
4. Using the same format and clipping or construction paper, make a design in which some of the ground is incorporated as figure.
5. Using the same format and clipping or construction paper, make a design in which figure and ground are reversible.

Specifications:

1. Materials:
   a. The 5- by 8-inch format suggested is convenient in size. It is large enough to work with freely but small enough to be adaptable to clipping materials. However, any reasonable size will serve as well.
   b. I suggest you clip your tones from magazine illustrations for two reasons:
      (1) It is important at this stage to allow yourselves the freedom, as you make your designs, of trying different tones, shapes, and positions in a free, experimental manner.
      (2) You can find a much greater range of tone qualities in magazine material than, say, in construction paper.
   c. When your composition is set, paste the clipping material neatly in place. Rubber cement or a good waterless paste makes a satisfactory adhesive. The only technical problems you will run into are those of precise clipping and neat pasting.
2. Presentation:
   a. Design an effective layout of these eight compositions and mount them on a sheet of illustration board.
   b. Use the general title, "Figure-Ground Organization," and title each composition to explain its significance.

Note: Do not try to make pictures in these compositions. It is essential for you to put your whole attention on the organization. Representational material can be used, but treat it as merely a shape with certain tone qualities.

3 FIGURE ORGANIZATION

We started the last chapter with a question: "How do we perceive form?" The answer was: "Through contrast in the visual field." The explanation of what that means introduced the idea of figure-ground pattern as the basic structure of our perceptions. We applied this to design organization, which gave us a framework for introducing the problems of form and composition.

Now we must ask another question, one that grows out of the first. "Why do we see the form we do?" This is not a facetious question. To say, "It is because the things we are looking at have that form," is not a full answer. Recall our discussion of the way light qualities in the visual field are transformed into an energy pattern in the brain. Our question could be restated this way: "Why does this energy pattern organize the way it does?" So far, we have discovered only what makes it break into the basic figure-ground elements. But to explain why the form is what it is, we must also find out why the figure elements organize as they do. This introduces the factors of attraction and attention value.

ATTRACTION AND ATTENTION VALUE

Before I define these terms, we should take another look at that energy pattern. It is something we are not at all conscious of as such, and yet it makes itself strongly felt. What happens is this: the dynamic condition in our brains and nervous systems becomes a subjective part of our visual field, making us respond to the objective field as if it contained dynamic forces. We feel these as different values of *attraction* and different degrees of interest or *attention value*.

Attraction means the direct pull resulting from a strong energy, either an area of intrinsically high physical energy, or a place where there is a strong contrast in visual qualities.

21

Attention value is more than that. It involves meaning. It calls up a more complex response, in that the values of association and past experience are also projected into the form.

If we are designing a poster, we try to give it strong attraction. We want to catch the eye in competition with the other attractions in the store window, or wherever the poster is to be seen. On the other hand, it need have only enough attention value to get across a simple and succinct message. If we are painting a picture, though, the problem is to charge all the forms with as much attention value as possible. We want it to hold up under prolonged and repeated study. We use attraction, too, as a tool in composing, but it is not the primary aim.

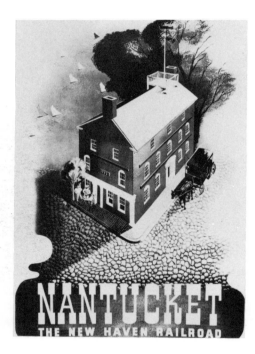

"Nantucket Poster," by Ben Nason. (*Courtesy of The Museum of Modern Art.*)

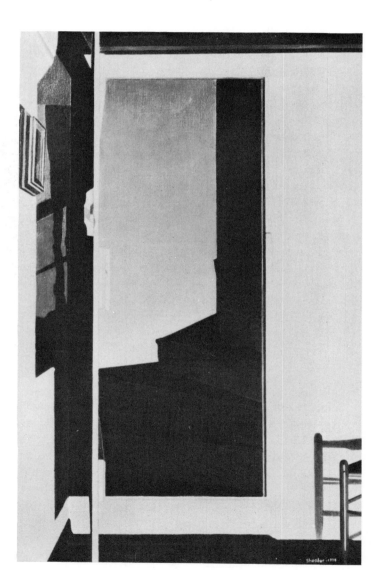

"The Upstairs," by Charles Sheeler, 1938. (*Courtesy of the Cincinnati Art Museum. Photograph by the artist.*)

22

I shall have more to say about attraction and attention value in themselves in the next chapter. Now consider how they affect the organization of figure elements.

THE ORGANIZATION OF FIGURE ELEMENTS

Spatial Basis for Grouping

Attraction has an effect not only on what we look at in a pattern first, but also on the way we organize the pattern. We shall make our discussion as simple as we can by speaking as if the forces of attraction were actually in the design itself. Here they have the effect of seeming to charge various parts of the pattern with different degrees of dynamic tension. (The tension is actually in us, remember.) A comparison with a magnetic field is helpful in visualizing the sort of thing I mean. The diagram shows how the lines of force arrange themselves. The lines might represent iron filings spread on a sheet of paper and held over the poles of a horseshoe magnet. If the distance between the poles is increased, there will be a point at which the tension breaks. The filings will then radiate symmetrically from each pole. Something very similar happens in the visual field. Put two square spots on a plain ground. Each has a certain strength of attraction from the contrast it makes with the ground. If the squares are close enough together, the resulting tensions in the field will tie the two spots together like the lines of magnetic tension. We will perceive one figure made up of two square elements. We call this effect of attraction on the field itself *spatial tension*. Now we move the squares farther apart. We will reach a point at which the two squares no longer organize together as a single complex figure spot. They will be seen as two completely separate figure elements.

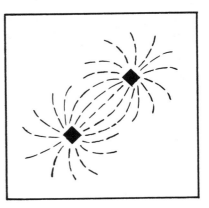

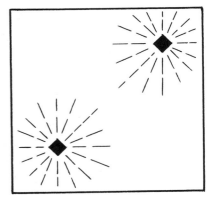

Magnetic tension.

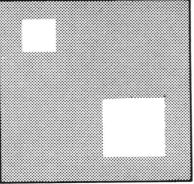

Spatial tension.

23

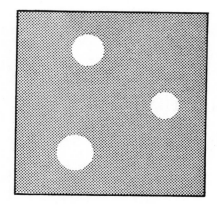

Effect of perception groups on spatial tension.

Spatial tension is reinforced in this respect by another psychological characteristic of our perceptions. Our minds are so constituted that we always try to group elements into larger units. The familiar constellations that men have found in the night sky are an illustration of this process. This peculiarity has a definite bearing on spatial tension. Wherever the larger pattern, made by individual units separated in space, is a "good" pattern (that is, of a nature to be easily perceived), the cohesion of spatial tension is reinforced. In the diagram, the three circles are separated by intervals that, by themselves, would break the intrinsic spatial tension. But because they are arranged in the easily perceived form of a triangle, we still unite them into a single perception group.

Where spatial tension is unassisted by an easily perceived larger grouping, it is directly proportional to the attraction of the elements. With strong attractions, quite an interval of space can be used and the spots will still group together; with weak attractions, the interval must be considerably smaller. This spatial tension, growing out of attraction and our tendency to see individual units in a patterned group, gives us one of the factors that determine what sort of form we perceive in a given field. It is an important resource in composing.

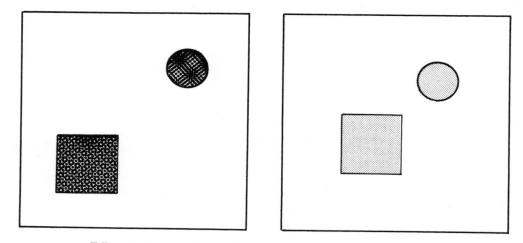

Effect of contrast on spatial tension.

There are other basic devices for achieving figure grouping that also deal with spatial relations. Consider our magnet again. You have probably played with one at some time or other. You know how firmly a nail or bar is held in place if laid across the poles. A closed and stable circuit is formed. The same kind of thing happens in the visual field. If two figure elements touch each other, they form a tight group of one composite figure. A number of basic possibilities are shown on the next page.

24

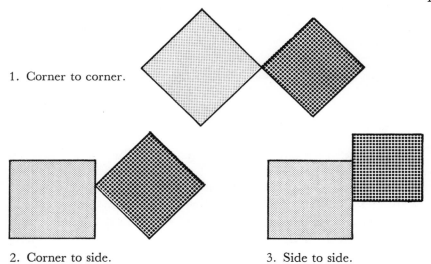

1. Corner to corner.

2. Corner to side.

3. Side to side.

Shapes that Overlap:

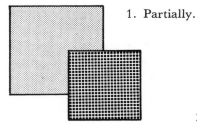

1. Partially.

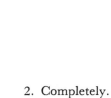

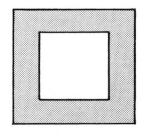

2. Completely.

Shapes that Interconnect:

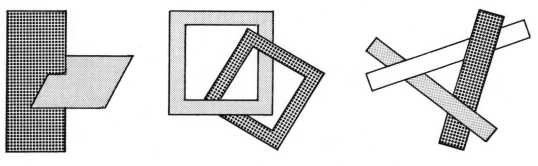

1. Interpenetrating.

2. Interlocking.

3. Interlacing.

(For the time being, we are thinking about two-dimensional organization. These ideas have three-dimensional counterparts that we shall take up later.)

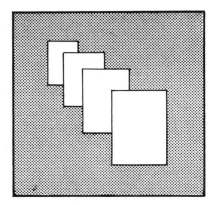

Depth through overlapping.

There is one important qualification to grouping by overlapping. Where a physically flat pattern has the illusion of depth, overlapping shapes may be separated in depth. In fact, overlapping is one of the basic *indications of space*. Although overlap may be used to create a sense of depth, it also produces a surface figure grouping. This is an important consideration in pictorial composition.

Likeness Basis for Grouping

The second organizing factor that is responsible for the kind of form we see in a pattern is *likeness*. I am using the word in its root sense: "The state or quality of being like; resemblance, similarity." (Webster's *Collegiate Dictionary*.) Whenever we can find a resemblance between things (any elements of similarity), we feel a relationship between them. Like spatial tension, such likeness also acts as a basis for grouping things in perception. This is a second basic tool in composing.

Perceiving likeness involves more than attraction. Attraction is largely a quantitative proposition. Likeness is qualitative. Here is where attention value and meaning come back into the picture.

This is a good place to consider how we find meaning in a visual pattern. It is simple to see when a shape in nature means a tree or a man. It is still simple when a representation on paper is made of those forms. If the real tree is on Lovers' Lane, it means more to us than just tree. If the painted tree reminds us of it, we project our associations into the picture. This kind of direct meaning and association is easy to understand. So is the use of shapes as symbols (if we understand the symbolism). Too often this is the only meaning people get out of visual arts. It is not the only kind there. It is not the only kind they respond to, even though they may be unaware of the fact.

Perhaps it seems simple-minded to say that a blue square means a blue square before it can have any other kind of meaning. Actually, this is meaning of the most fundamental sort. Everything else is added on through experience. The qualities that are perceived as blueness and squareness are given in the stimulus itself. In our ordinary daily business, we have to be more concerned with the sort of meaning things take on through experience. The roundness and color of an orange mean something good to eat. We pass over the actual perception of its visual nature for the perception of its use to us. So we get into a habit of treating most of our perceptions as shorthand symbols. A particular pattern in the visual field means chair. We sit on it without ever really seeing its particular shape, size, color, or visual texture. This works in most of our daily living. It does not work in designing or in appreciating designs. There we must register the actual qualities themselves. The intrinsic

26

meanings are just as important as those we add on from our reservoir of experience.

They are the basis of our perception of likeness. Two spots of red in a pattern, or two similar shapes, are tied together by similar meanings. We see a relationship, and this relationship affects the kind of form in which the figure organizes.

In the last chapter, we analyzed the different qualities we can perceive in a visual field. Any one or any combination of these can serve as the basis for likeness. We can outline the possibilities this way:

FORMAL FACTORS

1. Shape.

2. Size.

3. Position.

a. Direction.

b. Interval.

c. Attitude.

TONAL FACTORS

1. Achromatic-chromatic. (See Plate IV, 2*c*.)
2. Warm-cool. (See Plate VI, 1.)
3. Value. (See Plate VI,   )
4. Hue. (See Plate V, 1.)
5. Intensity. (See Plate V, 2.)

27

VISUAL TEXTURE

MEANINGS FROM EXPERIENCE

We can also have likeness in the meanings that are added from experience. So we complete our outline this way:

1. Representation   2. Association   3. Symbolism

The diagrams can only suggest the richness and subtlety in figure relationships that are possible.

You will notice that I slipped three new technical terms into the outline. Position is too general an idea to be of much use until we make it more precise. Since two things cannot be in the same place at the same time, we obviously cannot have an exact likeness in position. Position means more, though, than the exact place something has in the field. It also means its relationship to the structure of the field and to the observer. I shall go into the question of field structure more fully in the next chapter. For the moment, it is enough to say that it always has bottom, top, left, and right. This structure is, of course, relative to an observer. Most fields have also another set of directions—toward and away. They are even more obviously relative to an observer. Now let us see how objects in actually different positions in the field can still have elements of similarity dependent on their relationships to this structure.

28

DIRECTION means the relation of a shape to the basic directions of the field. Not all shapes have direction. It depends on whether there is a feeling of directional movement in the shape or not. A circle, for instance, is a static shape. An oblong rectangle, or any shape with a linear character, on the other hand, will have a feeling of movement along its long axis. Two or more such shapes in the field could have a similar direction if they were related to the field structure in the same way.

INTERVAL does not apply to the figure elements themselves. It is a quality they give to the ground. Since it is dependent on the position of the figure elements, this is the best place to discuss it. It means the size of the space between figure elements. We can make a likeness of interval by arranging the position of spots in the ground so that there are similar intervals between them.

ATTITUDE also involves the relationship of a shape to the structure of the field. A square and a diamond can be identical in everything but attitude. In fact, one of the essential things that makes the shape we call a diamond is the attitude. The corners have to relate to the up-down and left-right directions of the field. Again, shapes in different places can have likeness in their attitudes.

We can answer our question, "Why do we see the form we do?" on the basis of the actual pattern of visual stimulation and these two subjective organizing forces—spatial tension and likeness. The forces involved come from the pattern of nervous energy supplied in perception and operating through the two factors we have called attraction and attention value. We have had to discuss these problems separately for the sake of clarity. However, while every shape in the field will have specific qualities, there will almost inevitably be likenesses between some of these and the qualities of other shapes. Every shape will also have a spatial relation within the field and with other shapes. Both factors are always involved. They work together. We distinguish between them for clarity and control, but we cannot separate them in practice.

I want to caution you also against too simple and literal an interpretation of what we have said. If a pattern has any body, there will certainly be more than one way of seeing the figure relationships. This does not mean that they are confused or ambiguous. Take a simple example. Suppose we arrange a large white square close to a small black circle with a small white circle at a distance on a gray ground. The white square and black circle will group through spatial tension against the black circle. At the same time, the two circles will group through likeness in shape and size. The white square and white circle will group through tonal likeness. This is not a very complex pattern, but it shows three different figure relationships. With a really rich pattern, the variations are endless.

29

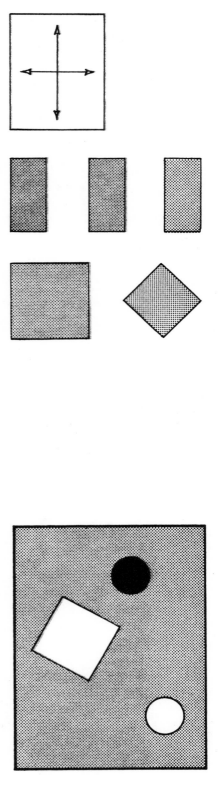

VARIETY IN UNITY

Up to this point, we have stressed the way visual perception works. I have taken pains to relate the problems of design organization to this process. Although we shall have to go back to physiology and psychology repeatedly as we get along in this book, it is time now to underline something that is basic in design, but accidental in general perception.

All we have said about figure organization is as true of general perception as it is of a designed pattern. The difference is that in a design these forces must make a unified composition. It is not enough merely to make clearly perceived forms in the field, although this is basic too. Particularly in drawing and painting the importance of clear figure-ground organization is tremendous, not in the result alone, but also in the development of our powers of conceptual visualization. Henry Schaefer-Simmern has a most provocative discussion of the part played by this developing ability to organize visual material in the growth of our creative powers.* But the designed pattern must also have the quality of an organic entity, complete and contained in itself. We have called this composition. It consists of a system of interlocking relationships that produce a *unity*. Spatial tension and likeness are two of the important relationships that contribute to the unity.

There is another side to this problem. Unity is not the only essential of design organization. To make a design effective, not only must we bind the parts together into an organic whole, but we must do it in an interesting way. That requires *variety*. Variety means three things:

First: In one sense variety is an inescapable part of the pattern. Contrast is variety, and we have already seen how our form itself is built out of contrasts. We have to control them, using the right kind and degree in the right place, to ensure unity. (Too much contrast, or the wrong kind, will destroy unity.) Still, contrast inevitably contributes variety to the pattern.

Second: Another kind of variety is implicit in what we have said about the different ways in which a figure pattern can be organized in perception. A rich pattern of spatial tension and likeness relationships imparts variety.

Third: There is absolute variety. This is like dissonance in music, something that is in complete contrast to the general system of relationships. Like dissonance, it adds spice to the ensemble.

* Henry Schaefer-Simmern, *The Unfolding of Artistic Activity.* University of California Press, Berkeley, Calif., 1948.

The ideal is symbolized in Hogarth's "line of beauty." This has been misunderstood as an S curve. What it really means is a line inscribed on a cone. As it moves in an ever-expanding spiral, each part is different from the part before, and yet in complete unity with it. The line, therefore, possesses absolute unity and absolute variety. That is what we have to aim at in designing.

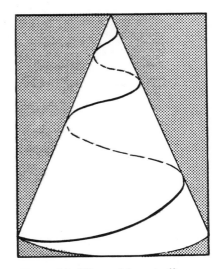

Hogarth's "line of beauty."

READING LIST

Kepes, Gyorgy: *Language of Vision*, P. Theobald, Chicago, 1944. Chapter 1.

Koffka, Kurt: *Principles of Gestalt Psychology*, Harcourt, Brace and Company, Inc., New York, 1935. Chapters 4, 5, and 6.

Köhler, Wolfgang: *Gestalt Psychology*, Liveright Publishing Corp., New York, 1947. Chapter 6.

Langfeld, Herbert Sidney: *The Aesthetic Attitude*, Harcourt, Brace and Company, Inc., New York, 1920. Chapter 7.

Thurston, Carl: *The Structure of Art*, University of Chicago Press, Chicago, 1940. Chapter 1.

PROBLEM II

Purpose: To find out how spatial tension and likeness can be used to control figure grouping.

Problems:

1. Spatial tension. Using 5- by 8-inch grounds and construction paper, make two compositions in which identical elements are grouped in contrasting figure organizations through spatial tension. I suggest that you limit the number of shapes in each pattern to from six to eight. They should all be identical in size, shape, and tone so that no organizing factor but spatial tension is involved. Do not use contact, overlapping, and so forth. The problem is to order the space intervals between the elements so that the pattern organizes as one or two or three figure groups, etc. Experiment to see just how large an interval you can use and still make the units group. Consider the effect of larger pattern units.

2. Likeness. Make four compositions using clipping material in which you explore different kinds of likeness between your elements as a basis for figure grouping. Some of the possibilities are:

Tonal	*Formal*	*Idea*
Chromatic-achromatic.	Shape.	Representation.
Warm-cool.	Size.	Association.
Value.	Position: direction,	Symbolism.
Hue.	interval, attitude.	
Intensity.		

Make as effective and interesting compositions as you can. Do not try to make mere demonstrations of one kind of likeness. More than one kind will almost certainly be involved. Remember what we said about how we can get different groupings in the same pattern on the basis of the various likenesses involved. At the same time, try to make a difference of emphasis in each composition. For instance, one might be based on two themes: a major achromatic theme and a chromatic one for variety. Another might emphasize visual textures (etc.)

3. Make an 8- by 10-inch composition using construction paper in which you use contact, overlapping, and interpenetration to organize your figure groupings.

Specifications:

1. Materials:
   a. Use a drawing paper of good weight or construction paper for grounds. Use colored construction paper and clipping materials to make your figure elements.
   b. Cut and paste your compositions as before.
2. Presentation:
   a. Design an effective layout of your seven compositions, and mount on a sheet of illustration board.
   b. Title the sheet "Figure Grouping," and title each pattern to explain its significance.

Note: Keep your designs abstract for the reason that I gave before. In using likeness in idea, there may well be some pictorial quality. Do not try to make conventional pictures, however.

4 MOVEMENT AND BALANCE

Unity and variety are the two concepts that guide us in analyzing what we mean by visual organization in design. Variety, by its very nature, does not lend itself to much generalization. The three points we made in defining it are about all we can say. Beyond that, we have to study the problem in the context of specific designs. This study is important; the imagination and sensitivity with which we handle variety has a lot to do with the quality of our designing.

The idea of unity, by contrast, has to be more fully developed. *Unity* is achieved by the organic knitting together of functional, visual, and expressive relationships to make our design a unique, self-contained thing. Figure-ground organization and figure grouping are important factors. They apply, however, to all perception. To give them the quality of unity in our designs, we need a more exact idea of the nature of unity.

THE NATURE OF UNITY

We shall get at it this way. I have used the expression "organic unity" several times. The word "organic" serves to underline the idea of a necessary and functional relationship between the parts and the whole. It is borrowed from the realm of living things, which always have this quality. An example from biology will help to focus the problem of unity in design.

Sir D'Arcy W. Thompson has written a fascinating book called *On Growth and Form.** In it he develops the thesis that natural forms are the expression of the balance between interior growth forces and exterior forces in the environment. His idea is that natural forms are, as it were, a material diagram of internal and external forces.

Jellyfish, for instance, are composed of liquid protoplasm. Being

*Sir D'Arcy W. Thompson, *On Growth and Form*, The Macmillan Company, New York, 1942.

33

liquids in a liquid environment, they show this balance very clearly. The internal forces are growth and surface tension. The latter is a physical force acting in both the organic and inorganic realms. The external forces are gravity and fluid friction.

A simple experiment will help to show how the physical forces involved operate. Suppose we take a tall glass of water. With an eye dropper, we deposit a drop of India ink on the surface. Now watch what happens. The heavier ink begins to sink. Surface tension keeps it from mixing readily with the water. Fluid friction flattens it out as it sinks into a disk that opens to form a ring. Little droplets break off around the rim. They sink until the friction causes them to form rings in turn. If the glass is tall enough, we can get several systems clearly defined, growing smaller as they descend.

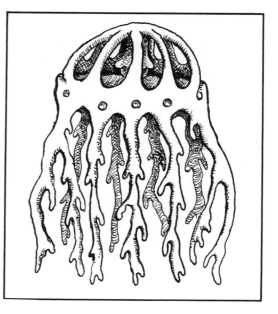

Ink rings and jellyfish

Compare the photograph of the ink rings with the jellyfish. Notice the obvious parallels between the two. The bell-shaped body of the fish is like the ink disk just before the center parts to form a ring. The protoplasm, having a higher specific gravity with more surface tension, reaches a balance before breaking into a ring. The tentacles hanging from the bell correspond to the system of falling droplets. A further remarkable parallel is the mode of reproduction in jellyfish. The infant grows on a tentacle in a manner similar to the formation of a smaller ink ring.

Thompson does not maintain that a purely physical explanation accounts for the jellyfish's growth. Rather, it is the startling parallel between the living form and one resulting from physical forces alone that is significant. The least that we can conclude is the close relationship between internal and external forces in shaping organic forms.

This example clarifies the problem of design unity in two respects. First, our visual response is one of perceiving all elements as parts of one whole. Second, the visual unity grows out of a deeper structural unity. Such structural unity is not a chance phenomenon, but the result of inevitable necessity. In nature this necessity is the interaction of growth forces and the shaping influences of the environment. In designing it is purpose finding formal expression in material through technique.

Now we can analyze the special characteristics of visual unity without losing our perspective on their place in the wider problem of design unity.

We shall find four qualities that must be present in any form that we see as a unity. These are:

1. A closed pattern of movement.
2. Balance.
3. Proportional relationships of size, number, and degree.
4. Rhythm.

In this chapter, we shall consider movement and balance; in the next, proportion and rhythm.

BACKGROUND OF VISUAL UNITY: Movement and Balance

The Structure of Our Visual Field

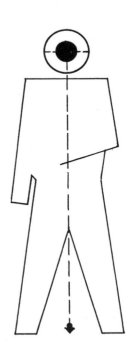

The space in which we live and our visual fields have structure. This structure is a function of our own nature. It is something we "add on" in the process of perception. For instance, the homogeneous field we spoke of in Chapter 2 is perceived as mist-filled space. It is three-dimensional with the potential axes: up–down, right–left, forward–back. These are ideas that depend on us as perceivers. Let us see how this state of affairs comes about.

UP–DOWN AND RIGHT–LEFT

Vertical and horizontal directions in our space field depend on our balance organs. Like the jellyfish (and everything else), we are subject to gravity. To stand or move, we have to keep our equilibrium; we have to keep our center of gravity within the base of support. (The principle is diagramed in the illustration). When we fail to do this, we fall down. That is unpleasant physically and psychically. (Falling and loud noises seem to be the two fears we are born with.) Consequently, balance and the visual signs that are correlated with it are very important to us. Two little organs in our inner ears, the semicircular canals, are the organic basis of balance. They

35

act as a sort of spirit level to tell us where our center of gravity is. As with a carpenter's level, the horizontal and vertical directions in space are the co-ordinates by which we judge this visually. These two directions take on a polarity in consequence. They become structural dimensions of our space and visual fields. The fun houses in amusement parks sometimes have rooms where diagonal planes have the illusion of being vertical and horizontal. If you have ever been in one, you know what a shock the fraud is to your sense of equilibrium. The trick is possible only because there is such an intimate connection between the perceived structure of our visual fields and the balance organism on which it rests.

FORWARD–BACK

But the homogeneous space of our fog has depth as well as vertical and horizontal directions. I made a note earlier of the significance of this direct perception of depth. It is one of the given things about space. When there are objects in the field, three other physiological processes reinforce depth perception. These are *disparity*, *accommodation*, and *convergence*, explained in the diagrams. The muscular responses and the patterns of nervous energy involved become an integral part of our perceptions.

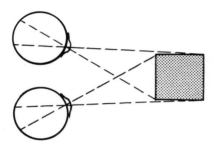

Disparity.

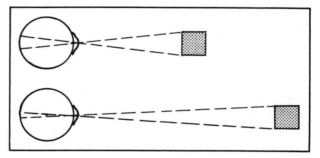

Accommodation.

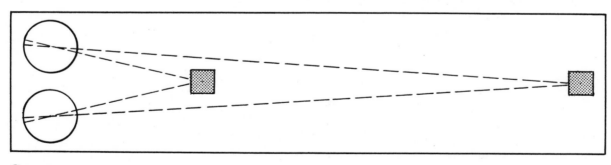

Convergence.

These three directions (vertical, horizontal, and depth), actually exist as polar forces in our organic and psychic make-up. We project them on space and on our visual fields. As a result, everything in the field is perceived in relation to this structure.

36

Our eyes receive stimulus from an angle of almost 180 degrees. We can sharply focus only about three degrees in the center of this angle, however. This is because of the structure of our retinas. Only the fovea, a small area on the axis of the lens, gives detailed perception. To perceive things of any size, we have to shift focus. The basis of our perceptions is actually a mosaic of many related sensation patterns plus the paths of association that have been stored up in our brains from past experience. *We see through the eyes, but we perceive with the brain.*

Notice the way your eyes behave in reading this line. They skip along, making several fixations at intervals. Focus at the beginning of a line and try to observe the end. You are aware of stimulation. You can distinguish fairly well the textural contrast between the type and the margin, but you can read only in the focused area. We "read" all forms this way. Our eyes behave somewhat after the manner of an insect's antennae. They explore one spot at a time. The comparison is not exact; the rest of the field is filled with stimulation too. But it is stimulation without satisfactory form. Still, it is very important. The half-seen forms and attractions clamor to be looked at. They keep our eyes on the move.

These two facts of our physiological-psychological make-up are important. Our need for balance and the necessity for movement in design are its corollaries. We shall consider first movement in design.

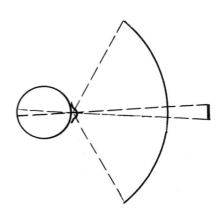

Acuity.

MOVEMENT IN DESIGN

Movement involves two ideas, change and time. The change may take place objectively in the field or subjectively in the process of perception, or both. In all cases time is involved. We have to distinguish between the objective and subjective aspects of movement in design. Some arts—movies, dance, and theater, for instance—involve objective movement. The pattern of such arts has an actual duration in time. Subjective movement is present in all perception. It is of greatest design significance, however, in the arts that are embodied in physically static patterns. It is with this subjective movement that we are now concerned.

I have just said that all perception involves movement. To contribute to design unity, it must have a special quality. It is not a simple question of getting movement into our patterns. We cannot avoid that. It is rather a problem of organizing the perception movements so that they will create a closed and self-sufficient cir-

37

cuit. There are no rules for doing this. The values with which we are dealing are completely relative. They depend on the character of the composition. The same shape and color will have quite different values in different fields or even in different parts of the same field. In the final analysis, composing movement depends on sensitive feeling and intuition. But, if we cannot lay down rules, we can isolate the factors on which our judgments rest. That is a good basis for developing and refining our sensibilities.

To control our subjective movement patterns, one sort of judgment we have to make is: what is the relative dynamic value of each element in the composition. That each element has some positive or negative dynamic quality, we are directly aware. What is the basis of these perceptions?

Dynamic Values in the Field

Relation of the Elements to the Field Structure

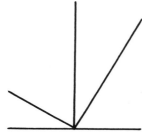

Because we project our own dynamic relation to gravity onto the field and its contents, they become dynamic. Horizontal elements are perceived as tending toward a static condition. Verticals are stable, but charged with a potential movement. Like us, they have to maintain their equilibrium or fall over. Diagonals, either on the surface or moving into depth, have the greatest activity. Forms take on these values partly from their linear outlines, partly from their dominant axis.

Attraction and Attention Value

The relative strength of attraction and attention value which a form possesses is an important factor in its dynamic value. Attraction and attention value depend on several elements within the form.

DEGREE OF TONAL CONTRAST

This may be expressed in any one of the tonal dimensions, for example, value or hue or intensity. More likely, it will involve a combination of dimensions. (Remember that contrast results from the tone of both figure and ground elements.)

38

DEGREE OF VISUAL TEXTURE CONTRAST

This is usually closely related to tone. Sometimes you may have visual contrast with unity of tone. This is often used for instance, in working with fabrics. A blue velvet, say, can accent a blue satin by its contrast in visual texture.

SIZE OF THE AREA

A discussion about the effect of size brings us squarely up against the relativity in our problem. You cannot generalize that big areas have stronger attraction than little ones, or vice versa. The attraction of a particular area depends on its qualities—as its tone, its shape, its position. These factors being constant, however, you can always tell exactly what the effect of size is in a given case.

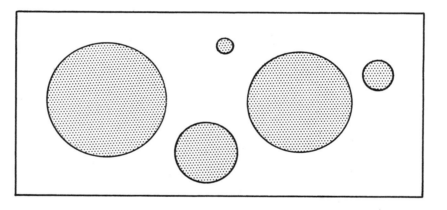

SHAPE OF THE FIGURE ELEMENT

This presents us with the same relativity. Three general factors influence the specific cases. To begin with, some forms, like the circle, are easier to see than others. (The psychologists have measured the amount of nervous energy it takes to see forms. The circle is the easiest, with other simple geometric forms following in close order.) This probably accounts for the strength of simple geometric shapes. On the other hand, good shapes (that is, shapes that are easy to perceive), which are also dynamic in line and position have a more powerful attraction than static shapes. Finally, shapes always involve some association or recognition value. Depending on what this is, it may well affect the dynamic quality. We shall discuss this at greater length in a minute.

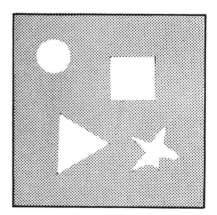

39

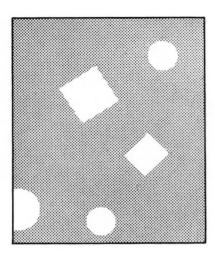

POSITION OF THE FIGURE IN THE GROUND

By virtue of the structure of our visual field, some parts of it are stronger than others. Experimental evidence shows that people tend to "enter" a two-dimensional pattern at a point to the left and a little above the geometric center. This is consequently a "strong" position. Positions close to the edges of the field are also likely to intensify the attraction of shapes. This is probably the result of spatial tension between the shape and the edge of the format. Breaking the format with the shape increases this effect. Bleeding an illustration, for instance, increases its attraction. Finally, the apparent weight of a figure, which is due to our projection of gravitational pull, also affects the value of position. It generally takes more space at the bottom of the field to balance a shape than it does at the top. This is the reason why we cut mats wider at the bottom than at the top.

DYNAMIC EFFECT OF BALANCE

I have pointed out that dynamic shapes are stronger than static ones. Balance has a special bearing on this. Compare the two pyramids in the illustration. The one poised on its apex is the same shape and is made up of the same·linear elements as the static one. Its dynamic relation to gravity, however, greatly increases its attraction.

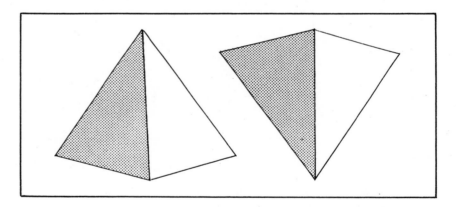

The Effect of Association and Representation

I said a moment ago that any shape will call up some association or recognition value. When this involves the idea of movement, it can considerably enhance the dynamic value of the form. Let us be specific. Take the well-known print, "Great Wave of Kanagawa," by Hokusai. We interpret the shapes he uses as waves. We immediately supply a rich content of movement made up of our direct experience with moving water plus the literary associations we have

40

with it. *Now this is very significant:* we can perfectly well have a shape that calls up this kind of background, but that is quite static in its direct formal values. Such a form will still be more dynamic than the first pyramid, for instance, which is static both in form and idea. In our print, though, the representational meaning and the direct formal values reinforce each other. The dynamic quality is greatly amplified. This is why a sensitive drawing is often more expressive of movement than an action photograph.

"Great Wave of Kanagawa," by Hokusai (1760–1849). (*Courtesy of the Metropolitan Museum of Art.*)

In judging the dynamic values of the elements in our composition, we shall have to consider some or all of these factors in changing combinations. Isolating them gives us a better basis for training our sensitivities. It also helps in the practice of composing to realize that we can increase or decrease the attraction of a form in these different ways. We may choose to do it, for instance, by manipulating the tonal contrasts, or by changing the size or position. The two things that guide our judgment are, first, the balance of the composition and, second, the pattern of subjective movement.

41

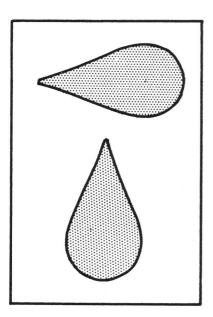

We have to make another type of judgment in controlling design movement. This has to do with the eye movements themselves. Writers on art and design usually speak as if the eye moved along the lines and contours in a composition like a train on a track. If we think back to our discussion of reading, we will see that this is not so. The eye always travels over the field in hops, stopping for a brief or long fixation where the attention and interest are caught. In reading, we are channeled to one sequence in the line and succession of lines. That is not true of design organizations. Our eyes can pick their own order of reading and their own rate. But they *are* "reading." At each stop, we evaluate what we are looking at. We get the idea content and the formal meanings. Among these are the dynamic meanings. We can tell perfectly well whether a line is intended to move up or down. We see one form as moving toward or away from another. One specific example will prove this statement. Consider the two teardrop shapes. They are identical except for their attitude. There is no question that both are dynamic. But the specific movement we ascribe to them will depend entirely on our associations. If we think of the horizontal shape as a spearhead, it is moving from left to right. Conversely, if we associate it with a streamlined automobile, it is moving from right to left. With the vertical form, as a drop of water, it is falling. As a tree, it is growing up. These evaluations are part of our perception. They have much to do with the expressive values we assign to the forms, and they exercise some influence over where we will look next.

What we have to do in composing these eye movements is not to be thought of as providing a system of tracks along which our eyes run. Rather, we have to distribute the attractions, the indicated directions, and the force of the various ideas of movement to create a closed and self-contained circuit. What this means is a distribution that keeps the eye moving within the format until attention is exhausted. There must be no leaks where the eye is allowed to escape from the pattern by accident. There must be a strong enough central attraction to balance peripheral attractions. Where the device of breaking the format is used, some equally strong counter-attraction must be provided. The very fact that we cannot coerce our eyes into any one-way circuit is one of the sources of richness in composition. A good movement design will provide a hundred ways of reading the circuit, all of them closed and interlocked systems. It is this factor that has much to do with the difference between a thin and a rich pattern. The beginner is content with a simple circuit, being glad to achieve a closed pattern. The master, however simple the apparent effect, works with a rich orchestration of movement pattern. Study the E. McKnight Kauffer magazine cover for '48 for an example of what I am talking about.

We have to consider the movement pattern in two ways. In some designs, it may be entirely on the surface. In others it is projected into the illusion of depth. (We are still concerned with two-dimensional compositions.) What I want to point out here is that the same element in the composition may have two values: one for surface movement; the other for movement in depth.

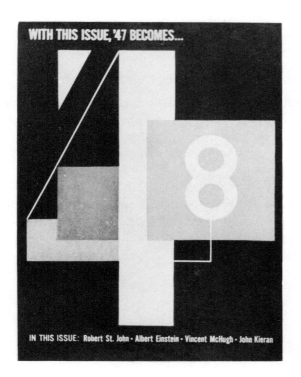

Cover Design for '48 Magazine, by E. McKnight Kauffer. (*Courtesy of the artist.*)

BALANCE

We have been unable to talk about the problems of movement in design without becoming involved in *balance*, the second condition of unity. We have analyzed the subjective basis of balance and seen why it is so essential in design. We know very well what it means in our own behavior. What, exactly, does it mean when we apply the term to design?

The center of gravity is still the basic concept, but we must obviously interpret it in a less literal way. The problem is not the equilibrium of a body in space, but that of all parts of a defined field. The easiest way of getting at this is to think of it as an equality of opposition. That implies a central axis or point in the field around which the opposing forces are in equilibrium. From this basic conception, three distinct types of balance organization evolve.

43

Axial Balance

Axial balance means the control of opposing attractions by an explicit central axis. This may be vertical or horizontal, or both.

SYMMETRY

Symmetry is the simplest form of this kind of balance organization. In an exactly symmetrical pattern, the elements are repeated in mirror image on either side of the axis or axes. It is the most obvious of all types of balance and, consequently, most lacking in variety. It is chiefly useful in decorative patterns or very formal compositions.

SYMMETRICAL FORM–ASYMMETRICAL COLOR

The pattern may be symmetrical in form, but asymmetrical in color. This is really using different principles for balancing the form and color. The severity of straight symmetry can be softened this way. The device is still chiefly useful for decorative pattern.

APPROXIMATE SYMMETRY

The two sides may be actually different in form but still similar enough to make the axis positively felt. Axial balance in painting is usually of this type. The Bellini "Madonna and Child" illustrated is a good example.

"Madonna and Child," by Giovanni Bellini (fifteenth century). (*Courtesy of the Metropolitan Museum of Art.*)

44

Radial balance means control of opposing attractions by rotation around a central point. This may be a positive spot in the pattern or an empty space. In the literal examples, two or more identical elements are rotated around this point. To visualize clearly what the principle means, contrast the radial pattern with a symmetrical pattern balanced on both vertical and horizontal axes. There are superficial resemblances. The difference is that a radial pattern must always have a movement around, while the symmetrical pattern is static. A very interesting variety of radial organization is achieved by using just two repeats of the motif. Radial balance is chiefly useful in decorative pattern making, although it occasionally crops up in architectural planning.

Occult Balance

Occult balance means control of opposing attractions through a felt equality between the parts of the field. It employs neither explicit axes nor central points. A "felt" center of gravity is, however, essential. It differs in principle from axial and radial balance in two ways. First, the absence of actual axes or focal center emphasizes the relativity of all the elements in the field. Second, it means opposing elements that are different rather than alike. For instance, we balance a small area of strong color in one part of the field by a large area of empty space in another. There are no rules for occult balance. It is all a matter of sensitive judgment of the varying attractions involved. This points up the close relationship between the problems of balance and movement. They can be separated only for discussion. When we are designing, the movement pattern is a part of our balance organization. The balance organization affects the movement value at every point.

45

Josef Albers has worked out a most interesting abstract pattern that points up very well what we have said about the nature of occult balance. He set himself an extremely exacting problem. We have explored the way the attraction values of different parts of a design field are related to the structure we project onto the field when we perceive it. Because of this relationship, the attitude of the format is most important in composing. Working in a shape in a vertical attitude presents quite different problems from composing in the same shape placed horizontally. Mr. Albers took the problem of creating a single pattern which would balance perfectly in all four possible attitudes of the format. The illustrations show the pattern turned through its four attitudes. The interesting thing to study is the way the attraction and movement values of the different parts of the form change from one attitude to another. No demonstration could better emphasize the complete relativity of the values of the different forms and their relationship to field structure.

It is quite apparent that occult balance is by far the most important kind, as well as the most difficult, since it gives greater freedom but demands greater control. Occult balance has an infinite range of variety and expression. You can do with it whatever your imagination and sensitivity can handle.

READING LIST

Brandt, Herman F.: *The Psychology of Seeing*, Philosophical Library, New York, 1945. Chapters 3 and 4.

Klee, Paul: *Pedagogical Sketch Book*, Nierendorf Gallery, New York, 1944.

Koffka, Kurt: *Principles of Gestalt Psychology*, Harcourt, Brace and Company, Inc., New York, 1935. Chapter 7.

Langfeld, Herbert Sidney: *The Aesthetic Attitude*, Harcourt, Brace and Company, Inc., New York, 1920. Chapters 5, 6, 7, 9, and 10.

Teague, Walter Dorwin: *Design This Day*, Harcourt, Brace and Company, Inc., New York, 1940. Chapter 13.

Composition balanced in four attitudes, by Josef Albers. (*Courtesy of the artist.*)

PROBLEM III

Purpose:

1. To give you a clear understanding of the three fundamental types of balance organization.
2. To explore the problems of movement and their relation to balance.

Problems:

1. Use a 5- by 8-inch ground and clipping material. At this point, it will be a good idea if you start making your own tones. (See the instructions for exploring pigments in Chapter 6.) I suggest that you still use the method of clipping and pasting in working out the designs, however. Make an abstract composition employing axial balance. Use a vertical or horizontal axis, or both.
2. Using a 5- by 8-inch ground and clipping material, make a composition employing radial balance.
3. On 8- by 10-inch grounds make three occultly balanced compositions as follows:
    a. One in which a pattern of linear movement is organized into a closed and balanced circuit.
    b. One in which a pattern of movement based on the axial movement of forms is organized into a closed and balanced circuit.
    c. One in which the movement of attraction from tone contrast, shape, size, etc., is organized into a closed and balanced circuit.

Specifications:

1. Materials:
    a. Use a drawing paper of good weight for grounds. If you make your own tones for clipping, paint areas approximately 6 by 6 inches on a paper that takes water color well without too much curling. It is a good idea to make some swatches with different textures. (You can do this with the brush, a sponge, by spattering, etc.) You may also exploit the different visual qualities of opaque and transparent paint. Be sure to make enough variations in value of your different hue mixtures.
    b. Cut your desired shapes from these color swatches, or use clipping materials as before. Organize and paste your compositions. (Be sure your swatches are flat before you try to cut shapes from them.)
2. Presentation:
    a. Design an effective layout for your five compositions and mount them on a sheet of illustration board.
    b. Title the sheet "Movement and Balance," and title each composition to explain its significance.

Note: Keep your designs abstract.

5 PROPORTION AND RHYTHM

I once started the discussion of the problems of proportion by asking my class what the word meant to them. The wheels of thought grind in silence. Finally, one brave girl came out with, "Oh, that is *A* is to *B*." Proportion and rhythm are perfectly familiar ideas, yet they are hard to define, particularly in their relationship to design. The dictionary gives us a point of departure. Webster's *Collegiate* defines *proportion* as, "the relation in magnitude, quantity, or degree of one to another; ratio"; *rhythm* as, "movement marked by regular recurrence; periodicity."

I think we will do better to let the significance of these two terms develop out of our discussion rather than to try now for formal definitions. But it is necessary to have a clear idea of the direction we are going to take. Ratio implies a comparison between like factors. The central idea in rhythm is expected recurrence. Now, let us trace these threads through the fabric of design.

ORGANIC BASIS OF PROPORTION AND RHYTHM

Like movement pattern and balance, these two qualities are always present in the organic forms of nature. They are expressions of the same internal and external forces of growth that we examined in the last chapter. We shall follow up this analogy. There is no better clue to their nature and function in design.

48

Wherever you start—at the atomic or the cosmic level, or any place between—proportion and rhythm are among the most striking characteristics of natural forms. Take two examples. The scientists are busy now hunting down new elements. It is still true that the original ninety-two make up the bulk of all the limitless substances we know. Difference in the proportion and arrangement of the same elements makes our world. If you burn hydrogen, a gas, in another gas, oxygen, the two unite to form water. The water molecule is always composed of two atoms of hydrogen and one of oxygen. In its liquid state, water is amorphous. If you solidify it, as in a snowflake, the intrinsic structure takes on visible form in which both proportion and rhythm are clear. Sir William Bragg wrote: "Order and regularity are the consequence of the complete fulfillment of the attractions which the atoms and molecules exert on one another."* Ice crystals are good mirrors of this fact. The basic unit is composed of four molecules whose structure is diagramed in the illustration. These tiny seed crystals combine in the endless patterns of snowflakes. The multiplicity of these forms is always a variation on one theme: the unity of the crystal structure. Ratio, you see, is imposed by the very nature of the form. It is expressed in the size and number of parts, in the angular degrees of the trunks and branches. These ratios, in turn, create rhythmic recurrences of shapes, sizes, and accents.

* Sir William Bragg, *Concerning the Nature of Things*, Harper & Brothers, New York, 1925.

Molecule of water.

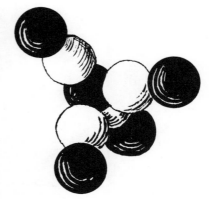

Molecular structure of ice crystal.

Complex ice crystal: snowflake.
(*Photograph courtesy of the Museum of Natural History, New York.*)

49

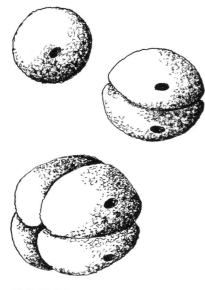

Cell division.

The other example, from the organic realm, is more complex. The same principle is still apparent. Life begins with a single fertile egg cell. It divides into two cells. They divide into four, and so on in geometric progression. In all higher organisms, this simple progression is not the whole story. At an early stage of growth, something new happens. Specialization for function takes place. The indwelling pattern in the chromosomes, like the intrinsic attractions of atoms and molecules, controls growth. It causes a greater division of cells in one direction, a slowing of growth in another. It changes the structure of the cells themselves to adapt them to function.

Study the monkshood leaf. Two specialized processes are evident to even casual inspection—the chlorophyll-bearing plates of surface cells that carry on the life function of photosynthesis, and the ribs and veins that support them. There is a clearly apparent ratio between these, and between the parts into which the structure divides. I have applied a little geometry to the photograph. By plotting the points along the main axes of the leaf at which branching takes place, we uncover the common ratio in all the parts. The recurrence of shapes and angles is obvious. Again, proportion and rhythm are revealed as the inevitable expressions of growth.

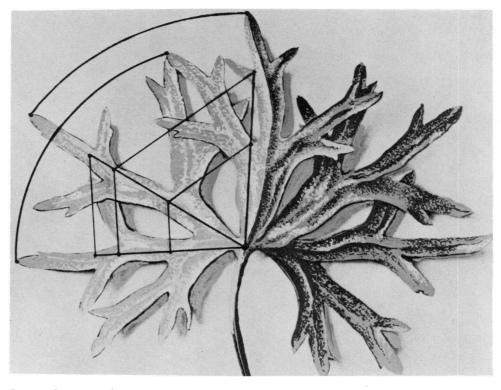

Geometric analysis of a monkshood leaf.

50

There is a lesson in this for us to take to heart. Ratios are mathematical concepts. They deal with magnitude, number, and degree. We shall shortly explore the ways of analyzing and expressing them. It is easy to lose the significance of ratio and rhythm in the fascination of their mathematical and geometric structure. What our examples should teach us is that in design, as in nature, *they are meaningful only when they express functional necessities.* We cannot talk about good proportion in the abstract. The idea is meaningless without the further question, "Good for what purpose?" In designing, our purposes will be manifold and complex. But they can always be thought of from two points of view. One determinant will be structural and functional; the other, expressive. There need be no conflict between these. Louis Sullivan's dictum, "Form follows function," is the ideal toward which we aim, an ideal which nature exhibits in all her work.

There is, of course, a difference in emphasis depending on what we are designing. Three-dimensional designs, by their very nature, impose more rigorous material and technical limitations than do two-dimensional ones. They force us to deal with actual weight and stress and with the problems of joining one piece to another. In the physical sense, two-dimensional design, a picture or a page layout, allows a freer emphasis on purely aesthetic determinants for our ratios and rhythms. Even there, however, the question of whether they are good or not is more than a problem of mathematics. In the final analysis it is a question of expression. Mathematics and geometry are our tools for analyzing and stating the structure of ratios. They can never answer the question of rightness and suitability to purpose.

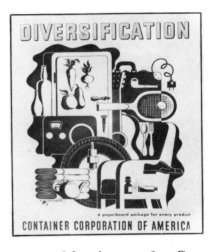

Advertisement for Container Corporation of America, by Cassandre. (*Courtesy of the Container Corporation of America.*)

Furniture by Charles Eames. (*Courtesy of the designer.*)

51

Consider two examples from this angle. First, compare the Whitestone bridge with that designed by Robert Maillart at Salginatobel, Switzerland. In both, the functional engineering problem has dictated the form. The ratios embodied in their parts have a strictly structural basis. The revealing contrast between the two designs is the way the materials chosen determine what is "good" proportion. The great piers and steel cables of the Whitestone bridge grow organically out of one set of limitations and potentialities. The reinforced concrete forms of Maillart's bridge speak another language. This structure is significant in another way. If we think of the usual form of concrete bridge with which we are familiar, Maillart's design seems strangely fragile, almost insubstantial. He was able to construct his form with such economy of means because he was the first to use the slab of the roadbed as a structural part of the design. In his bridge it is not simply a bearing surface for traffic, adding its inert weight to the structural parts. It is an integral working member of the system. Siegfried Giedion says of it in *Space, Time, and Architecture:* "Thus Maillart resolved bridge-building into a system of flat and curved slabs so juxtaposed as to achieve a positively uncanny counterbalance of all stresses and strains arising between them."* "Good" proportion in these terms

* Siegfried Giedion, *Space, Time, and Architecture,* Harvard University Press, Cambridge, Mass., 1941.

Bridge at Salginatobel, Switzerland. Designed by Robert Maillart. (*Courtesy of Dr. Siegfried Giedion. Photograph by D. Mochol, Schiers, Switzerland.*)

Whitestone Bridge, New York. Aymar Embury II, architect; Allston Dana, engineer. (*Courtesy of the designers. Photograph by Richard Averill Smith.*)

Louis XIV armchair, about 1690. (*Courtesy of the Metropolitan Museum of Art.*)

is something quite different from the good proportion of conventional ferroconcrete construction.

Second, compare the two chair designs, one Louis XIV, the other Louis XV. In both functional relation to the scale of the human body was a determining factor. In both the influence of material and structure is apparent. Beyond this the expressive purpose (the style) of the two periods is clear. Most design problems have more than one solution. Structural and aesthetic requirements can be met in several ways with equal effectiveness. Faced with choices, the designer will always judge as "good" those shapes and ratios that express the form ideals of his time and social environment. The Louis XIV design expresses the formality and ritual that were the temper of the Sun King's court. The whole emphasis is on display at the expense of comfort. The qualities of the Louis XV design are comfort, informality, and feminine elegance. If we knew nothing else of these two periods, the chairs would tell us a good deal about the values of their respective societies.

Louis XV side chair by Jacques Marin, about 1743. (*Courtesy of the Metropolitan Museum of Art.*)

53

One more idea before we get involved with our analytical tools. It is implicit in what we said above that proportion relationships must be felt if they are to operate visually. That they can be demonstrated by analysis is not enough. Because this is true, we might ask: "Why bother with mathematical and geometric analysis at all? Will it not simply get in the way of our intuitive feelings?" If we use it in the right way, the answer is "no," and for this reason. There is no conflict between feeling and mathematics. Some of you may be inclined to quarrel with that statement. Unfortunately, most of us are taught mathematics in a vacuum, divorced from its human context. We never realize that it is a language invented by the human mind to express the kinds of relationship we can perceive. It is true that, given the language, we can use it to formulate possible relationships never before perceived. That is exactly what has happened again and again in the history of science. It is not true that there is any conflict between this language and our feeling for relationship. How could there be? After all, our minds are products of the same forces of growth that operate in the rest of nature. When we analyze ratios mathematically, we are only responding totally to the stimulus. We are bringing the force of our reasoned perceptions to the aid of our direct sensibilities. This is the way of growth. This is the best method for sharpening and refining our sensibilities. As in every other aspect of life, there will be something left over which we cannot analyze—some felt, but irrational relationships. This need not worry us. Look at the monkshood leaf again. Although the ratios my analysis reveals are certainly there, they are not expressed with any mechanical accuracy. The intention, as it were, is clear, but the forms are full of slight variation, unexpected caprice within the expected rhythm. Even in our age of machine tools and mass production, where precision is the cardinal virtue, we can not and do not want to eliminate this felt but indefinable something that contributes so much to the vitality of our work.

ANALYZING PROPORTION AND RHYTHM

I have taken so much time to establish the real nature of proportion and rhythm and of our means for analyzing them for two reasons. They are the Scylla and Charybdis between which we have to steer. Without some means for making concrete statements about felt ratios, we are reduced to airy generalizations. On the other hand, a literal dependence on mathematics and geometry results in mechanical sterility. If we understand that these aids are tools for clarifying our understanding and sharpening our sensibilities, I think we can steer the course safely.

Simple Numerical Ratios

Simple ratios, such as 1:1, 1:2, 2:3, 3:4, and so on are directly perceived and felt. They can be expressed between any comparable qualities of form and tone. For instance, a rectangle with a long side twice the length of the short expresses this kind of ratio. Such ratios are not particularly subtle or dynamic, but they have their own simple strength. The concept of ratio is often restricted to comparisons of length and volume. This is too narrow an application. The same principle is equally valid wherever we have comparable qualities. In tone contrast, for instance, if value A is one step lighter than value B and two steps lighter than value C, we have a double ratio. The comparison from A to B to C is 1:1; from A to C it is 1:2.

It does not take long, however, to arrive at ratios that may be perfectly good mathematical statements, but that are too complex to be felt. The ratio 13:19 makes mathematical sense; but it is questionable whether one could make any design sense of it. If one did, it would be because it so closely approximates 2:3. We would really be working with the nearest simple ratio that can be felt.

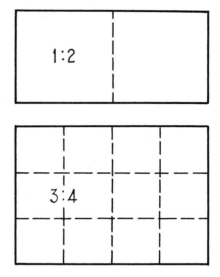

Values of the Summation Series

There is another and much more interesting set of numerical ratios. It develops out of what is known as the *summation series*. If we add one and two, the first two whole numbers, their sum is three. The series builds by adding the sum of each preceding two numbers. So we get the series, 1–2–3–5–8–13–21–34–55–89, and so on, to infinity. The particular property of this series is that it gives us the closest whole number approximation to mean and extreme ratios. Let us see what that means. We can express it algebraically this way: $A:B::B:C$. If we translate this into values from the series, we get: 1:2::2:3 or 2:3::3:5. From algebra we remember that the product of the means must equal the product of the extremes. We see, therefore, that our equations are inaccurate. In the first, the means are one more than the extremes; in the second, one less. This same error of one runs through successive steps of the whole series (21:34::34:55, or 1155=1156; 34:55::55:89, or 3026=3025, etc.). At the beginning the error is great. As the series progresses, it becomes very small indeed. The interesting thing about such ratios is that they involve a definite rhythmic progression. The same relationship is repeated in each increase of magnitude. This is much richer in its possibilities than a simple numerical ratio. We can apply the idea in the same fashion as our 1:2 and 2:3 ratios to lines, areas, or any other commensurate element in the composition.

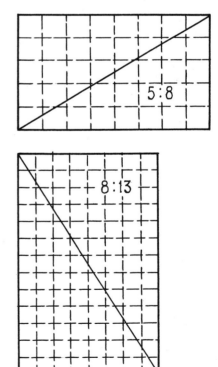

55

This set of ratios has a special significance because of its frequent occurrence in nature. If we take the pineapple illustrated, the arrangement of the scales makes two sets of spiral valleys around the form. One of these curves is steep and spirals in a counterclockwise direction. The other is much longer and more gradual, spiraling clockwise. If we count these two sets of spirals around the form, we shall find that their numbers correspond to two succeeding values of the summation series. If we count the scales in each type of spiral, their totals will correspond to values from the series. These spiral forms occur over and over in nature. Pine cones, sunflowers, and many flower and petal arrangements repeat them. They are true logarithmic spirals. This is but another evidence that the process of growth inevitably expresses itself in ratio and rhythm.

Logarithmic spirals in a pineapple. (*Photograph by Edith Levy.*)

56

The third possibility for analyzing felt ratio relationships is geometry. Its most fruitful application, therefore, is to geometric forms, although its significance is not limited to them. Traditionally, there have been two approaches to this method. Architects and painters have often used a framework of related geometric shapes and construction lines to provide regulating lines for their compositions. There is a very interesting example of this in Dürer's engraving "Melancholia." Looking at it one day, I was intrigued to figure out the significance of the magic square he incorporated in the upper right-hand wall. Whatever iconographical meaning it might have, I wondered if it might not also have some structural significance. The illustration presents my analysis. If we connect the numbers in sequence with straight lines, a radially balanced geometric pattern results. Taking the middle of each square as the focus of the numeral, the format falls exactly within this pattern. Its ratio is thus 3:4. All the main lines in the pattern will be found to fall either upon or parallel to the geometric regulating lines. The internal evidence of the pattern seems to indicate strongly that Dürer used this device to guide his composition and to help achieve this ratio and rhythm.

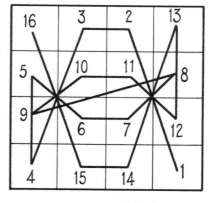

Magic square.

"Melancholia," by Albrecht Dürer, sixteenth century. (*Courtesy of the Metropolitan Museum of Art.*)

Other frequent devices of this sort are the square within the circle, the pentagon, the hexagon, and the five- and six-pointed stars related to them. All these rely on the intrinsic ratios developed by the relationships between simple geometric shapes and their subdivisions.*

* Walter Dorwin Teague has some very interesting diagrams showing the application of these schemes to historic examples of architecture. See *Design This Day*, Chapter 10.

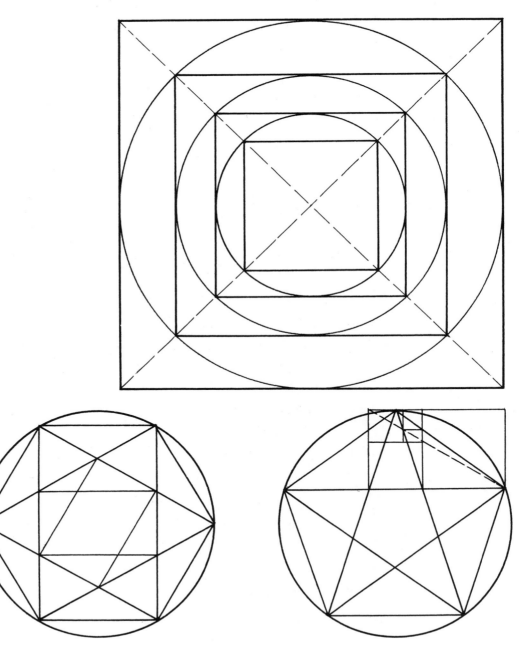

The other approach, which we believe was used by the Greeks during the great period of the fifth century and which has been reformulated by Jay Hambidge, is *dynamic symmetry*. I do not wish to get tangled in the complexities of this theory. It is worth while, however, to develop a few of the main demonstrations. To me, the most interesting is the golden-mean rectangle, or what Hambidge calls the whirling-square rectangle. Its interest lies in the way it ties up with the summation series ratios.

The Greek interest in mathematics was mainly philosophical. They objected to fractions on theoretical grounds, but they invented geometry. Whatever use they made of dynamic symmetry must have been based on the simple operations that one can accomplish with a string, a straightedge, and a pair of points. If we keep this in mind in our own analysis, we can guard against the pitfall of distracting complexities arising from mathematical translations.

GOLDEN-MEAN RECTANGLE

If we use the diagonal of half a square as radius, and circumscribe a half circle on the square, a very interesting set of ratios evolves. The segment of the diameter outside the square and the base of the square will be in extreme and mean ratio, *A:B::B:AB*. If we complete a rectangle on this base line, it will consist of the square and another rectangle similar to the parent rectangle. The sides of these shapes are in extreme and mean proportion, *A:B::B:C*, *C* equaling *AB*. The term "whirling square," comes from the further development of this shape. If we draw the main diagonal and a line from one corner at a right angle to it, we have regulating lines for dividing the shape into an endless sequence of progressively smaller square and similar rectangular areas. The squares rotate around the crossing of the two diagonals. If regular arcs, using a corner as center and a side as radius, are swung in each square, they will join to form a true logarithmic spiral. The effect of the repetition of the same extreme and mean ratio, interlocking the parent shape and all its subdivisions with nothing left out, is the basis for calling this form dynamic.

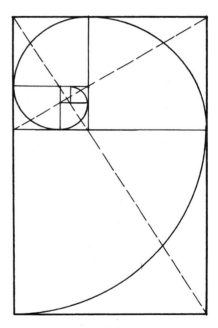

Development of the golden-mean rectangle.

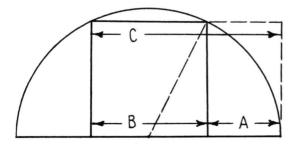

Construction.

59

ROOT-FIVE RECTANGLE

Now, go back to the square in the semicircle for a moment. If we complete a rectangle on the whole diameter, using the side of the square for the width, we have a new dynamic shape. It is made up of a square flanked by two golden-mean rectangles, but it has special properties of its own. If we draw the diagonal of this shape and a line at right angles to it from one corner, we have regulating lines for its dynamic division. Extend the shorter line and it will become the diagonal of a similar rectangle which is one-fifth the total area. We can carry on this development also, subdividing the shape into similar areas with nothing left over. Since this shape includes both the square and the golden-mean rectangle, the relationships between the subdivisions are very close.

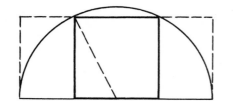

Construction.

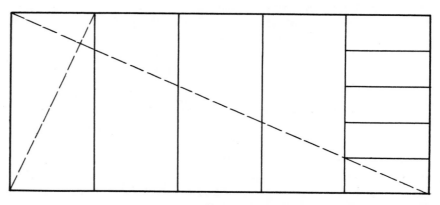

Development of the root-five rectangle.

Intrinsic Geometric Ratios

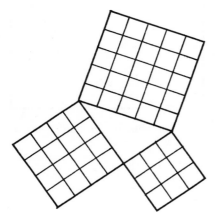

With some temerity, in view of the weight of authority behind these two approaches to geometric proportion, I want to suggest that the most fruitful idea they embody is the intrinsic ratio between sides and diagonals of rectangular shapes. The foundation for this is the Euclidean theorem that the square on the hypotenuse of a right triangle is equal to the sum of the squares on the two sides. This is always true, regardless of the shape of the triangle. In other words, there is always a fixed ratio between these three magnitudes. Applied to geometric analysis, it means that we can always repeat ratios in rectangular shapes by the use of parallel and right-angular diagonals. It is true that shapes other than the golden-mean and root-five rectangles will not subdivide with the complete rhythmic repetition these two shapes exhibit. On the other hand, there are many situations where neither of these shapes will apply that we can analyze by the more general principle.

60

Consider its virtues. In the first place, given any rectangular shape, we can repeat the ratio between its sides by drawing lines that intersect on the diagonal parallel to two adjacent sides. Smaller shapes can be constructed within the rectangle this way. By extending the diagonal, larger shapes can be formed on it. This insures similar shapes, repeating the original ratio. It does not establish any commensurate ratio between the areas. On the other hand, if we swing the length of either side across the diagonal, the intrinsic relationship between sides and diagonal will give us areas with related ratios. This principle can be repeated endlessly.

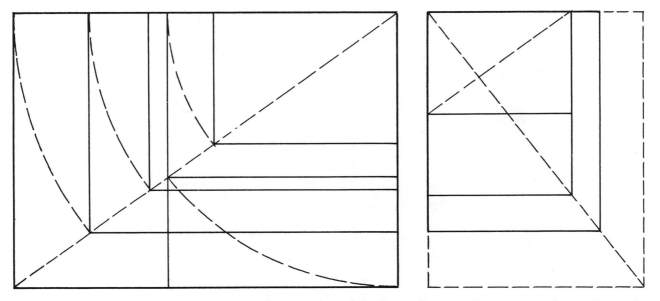

Construction of similar and proportionate rectangles on diagonals.

The same idea can be applied to triangles whether they are right triangles or not. By another theorem, all triangles with equal angles are similar in shape. Therefore, given any triangle, we can construct new similar triangles by drawing lines parallel to the sides. Related areas will evolve from cutting the long side with the length of either of the other sides and completing the figure from this point.

This device provides us with a ready tool for transposing any linear ratio into either larger or smaller magnitudes. To take a homely but troublesome problem, suppose we want to divide a line into thirds. Suppose, further, that the division does not work out on our scale rule. The diagram is much clearer than description. You can easily see the principle. It is very useful, for example, in scaling up a layout for reproduction. Its possibilities for building rhythm-producing ratios between different elements in our compositions are obvious.

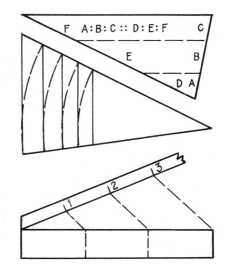

A second virtue is the way in which any rectangular form can be developed to give similar shapes embodying the same ratio. The practical procedure is simple. All we have to remember is that rectangles with parallel sides will be proportional if their diagonals are either parallel or at right angles to one another. The illustration analyzes a page layout from *Vogue* magazine. The basic ratio here was set by the size and shape of the page. This is characteristic of limitations we often meet that make the dynamic rectangles of little use. I shall not describe the analysis since it is clearer in the illustration. The point I want to emphasize is the flexibility of this method. It can be used effectively where neither straight geometric regulation nor orthodox dynamic symmetry will apply.

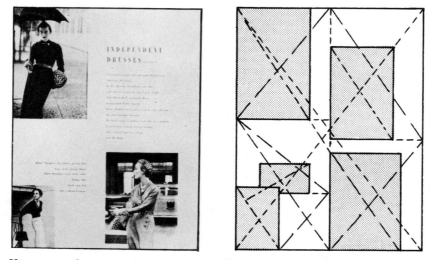

Vogue page layout and construction. (Reprinted from *Vogue*, September 1, 1949. Copyright 1949, *The Condé Nast Publications, Inc.*)

These geometric tools work only for shapes and sizes. The numerical ratios, by contrast, are valid for any comparable qualities in a design. They should be used to help us construct the specific relationships we want either for structural or expressive purposes, and as a test of our intuitive judgments. In the final analysis the ratio must be in our mind's eye if it is to be felt. No mechanical system can guarantee that.

RHYTHM

So far in our discussion we have suggested that rhythm is closely tied up with ratio. We have seen it evolve from the inevitable growth ratios in nature. It is now time to be more specific about what we mean and about how this works.

Rhythm differs from simple repetition in this respect: It is *expected* recurrence. The term "rhythm" is borrowed from the related art of music. There, the sequences of tones follow each other in time. In physically static visual designs, the movement is subjective, but none the less real. The simplest example would be a regular series of shapes with the same interval between them. (Notice that it requires three repetitions to establish this interval. In other words, three terms is the smallest number with which we can build a sequence.) A colonnade, with the repeated beats of solids and voids, presents such a pattern. It creates a rhythm. We cannot change the size of the columns or the space intervals without disturbing our expectation of recurrence.

Sequence of Progression and Alternation

Such a simple rhythm, however, is only the beginning of the possibilities. In the first place, there are two other kinds of sequence. Instead of repeating the same unit or interval, we can introduce regular progression in one or both terms. We can increase the height or width of the units by a proportionate amount or change the intervals in a like manner. The idea can be applied to any of the visual dimensions, such as shape, size, tone, visual texture. The result is an acceleration or retarding of the movement with a more complex kind of rhythm. Or an alternation between two motifs can be used effectively. Instead of the same form, we can alternately repeat two or more contrasting forms, colors, or intervals. The result is again a more complex rhythm.

Progression.

Alternation.

These possibilities for creating visual rhythm are still obvious. That they are highly effective almost any natural form testifies. Study the illustration of the flower form and see how many different rhythms of repetition, progression, and alternations are present!

Occult Rhythm

But the most exciting possibility is much subtler. There is a similarity here to the differences between obvious and occult balance. Rhythm, too, can be, as it were, occult. What we mean by this is that not merely obvious forms or colors, but also whole systems of relationships are repeated. This illuminates the subtle connection between rhythm and ratio. A whole composition can be thus unified by interlocking systems of ratio so that the same rhythm is endlessly varied in all the elements.

An example of this, in which the rhythm is expressed chiefly in sizes and shapes, is the Parthenon. Its composition brings us back

Visual rhythm in a passion flower.

to geometry. It is significant that the Doric temple plan was set by the time Ictinus and Callicrates designed their masterpiece. We can trace the progressive search for the expression of just such perfect rhythm through the sequence of temples in Sicily to the Parthenon. The architect's whole inventive genius was devoted to the problem.

Study the façade of the Parthenon. The enclosing form envelope, determined by the width of the pediment and the height to the top of the entablature, is a golden-mean rectangle. Remember that the generating parts of this form are a square plus another golden-mean rectangle. The main horizontal division, the bottom of the architrave, comes exactly at the intersection of the diagonals of the whole shape and those of the squares constructed in either end of the shape. This line divides the whole shape into large squares with a vertical golden-mean rectangle below and a small, central square flanked by two horizontal golden-mean rectangles above. The construction lines indicate the location of the other major horizontal and vertical space divisions. The same ratios, expressed in the square and the golden-mean rectangle, pervade every detail from the whole to the smallest part. The result is a structure tied together by the same organic rhythm of growth that the forms of nature have. The Parthenon works with visual rhythms of shape and size ratios. The same subtle organization can be expressed in all the visual qualities of a design.

Geometric analysis of the Parthenon.

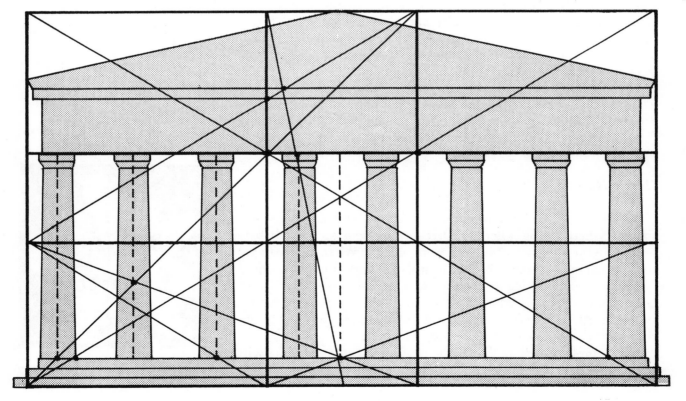

DOMINANCE AND SUBORDINATION

This idea brings us to one final point. The inevitable complement of such a pattern of rhythm is proportion in the relative importance of its various elements. Even in a simple colonnade, its symmetrical form results in dominance of the axis. Where the pattern is rich in varied rhythms, this principle of proportion in value, by which some parts are given *dominance* and others *subordinated*, is of the greatest importance. It is easy to see the relationship this bears to movement circuits and balance. Once again we meet the inevitable relatedness of every part of the design problem with every other part. Designing is like swimming. You can analyze kick, stroke, and breathing. You can practice them up to a point in artificial segregation on dry land. But if you are going to swim, they are all part of one operation. Each movement contributes to the unity that swimming is. You cannot understand those movements, let alone master them, except in relationship. Movement pattern, balance, proportion, and rhythm all contribute to the unity of a design. We can get a clearer comprehension of them through analysis, but we will master them only by actually designing, by working with all the factors in relationship.

READING LIST

Bragdon, Claude: *The Beautiful Necessity*, A. A. Knopf, New York, 1922. Essay on "The Arithmetic of Beauty."

Colman, Samuel, and C. Arthur Coan: *Nature's Harmonic Unity*, G. P. Putnam's Sons, New York, 1912.

Colman, Samuel, and C. Arthur Coan: *Proportional Form*, G. P. Putnam's Sons, New York, 1920.

Graves, Maitland: *The Art of Color and Design*, McGraw-Hill Book Company, Inc., New York, 1941. Chapter 8.

Hambidge, Jay: *The Elements of Dynamic Symmetry*, Brentano's, New York, 1926.

Teague, Walter Dorwin: *Design This Day*, Harcourt, Brace and Company, Inc., New York, 1940. Chapters 9, 10, and 11.

PROBLEM IV

Purpose:

To introduce the problems of proportion and rhythm. This problem is inevitably less comprehensive than the preceding ones. The relation of proportion of function, for instance, cannot be included. What we shall do is to introduce two characteristic approaches to the purely formal aspect of proportion and rhythm. We can call these "From the whole to the parts," and "From the parts to the whole." In some design problems, you will have a given area to divide into related parts. In others, you will have given units to fit into a certain space. These approaches to proportion and rhythm are, of course, closely related, but they present characteristic differences. In one, all the parts grow out of the parent area by division. In the other, you have two sets of determining factors, the format area, and the shapes to be composed.

Problems:

1. From the whole to the parts:
   a. Using an 8- by 10-inch format, divide the area into a composition of proportionate and rhythmical parts. Use only straight vertical and horizontal lines. Let all the parts be closed areas. Execute this composition in ink line of uniform weight throughout.
   b. Work up this same composition in color. Let each area come into direct contact with its neighbors. (The only lines will be the contrast between one color area and another.) You will find that the control of tone contrasts and attractions has to be very sensitive to maintain good proportion and rhythm relationships. This problem dramatizes the point made in our discussions that proportion is much more than a question of linear and area relationships.
2. From the parts to the whole:
   a. Using an 8- by 10-inch format, make a linear composition in which you start with two or three key shapes placed in relation to each other and to the format. Develop your proportions and rhythms by adding new shapes as the composition requires. Any type of line may be used, but be sure to include only closed areas. Pay attention to the negative ground shapes and areas. Execute your design in uniform ink line.
   b. Work up the same composition in color as before.

Specifications:

1. Materials:
   a. I suggest that you study your linear compositions at full scale on tracing paper. When they are set to your satisfaction, trace all four patterns (two of each design) well laid out on a sheet of illustration board. This makes an excellent surface to work on, both in ink and in water color.
   b. Opaque water color or poster color will be the most satisfactory paint.
2. Presentation:
   Title the whole sheet "Proportion and Rhythm." Title each group respectively: "From the whole to the parts," and "From the parts to the whole."

6 COLOR: Pigment and Tone Control

Visual contrast is the basis of form perception. We defined the tonal dimension of light and pigment in which contrast is expressed in Chapter 2. Control of these contrasts is basic to visual organization. It is now time for us to explore more fully how we can do this. We shall confine our attention in this chapter to pigment control.

I believe the soundest approach to this problem is through the material cause. We actually control tone contrast in two ways: either we select materials for their intrinsic tones and combine them on this basis, or we apply pigment in the form of paint, dye, and so forth, to get the effect we are after. Pigments are, therefore, basic materials in designing. We need an intimate and sympathetic understanding of their nature if we are to use them creatively.

The factors we are about to study are often presented in the form of a theory or system of color. This procedure has its advantages in simplicity and coherence. But I believe its tendency to divorce the structure of tone mechanics from its organic basis in the nature of pigment overweighs these virtues. Although we shall have to state our principles with more qualifications, I believe it is sounder and more craftsmanlike to study the problem directly through pigment materials themselves.

TONE CONTROL

We defined the *tonal dimensions* of reflecting surfaces as value, hue, and intensity. Let us consider the ways of controlling them.

67

Controlling Value

White pigment gives us one extreme of the value range; black, the other. By mixing them in varying proportions, we get a wide range of perceptibly different grays between. All these tones are achromatic. But value is a dimension of chromatic tones too. Every pigment has an intrinsic coefficient of reflection, that is, value. It ranges from very light for a yellow like barium sulphate to very dark for a pigment like burnt umber. When we mix pigments of different value, the resulting tone will fall somewhere between them. Thus we have four possibilities for mixing pigments to control the value of our tones:

See Plate I, 3
page 87.

1. Adding white raises the value.
2. Adding black lowers the value.
3. Adding a contrasting gray (both black and white) raises or lowers the value.
4. Adding a pigment of different value raises or lowers the value.

Note this fact: *we cannot change the value of a chromatic pigment without changing other tonal dimensions at the same time.* This is one of the intrinsic facts about the nature of pigments that we need to understand. We must know how it works.

1. Adding black, white, or gray introduces an achromatic component. The value will be changed and so will the intensity level. The resulting tone will be lighter or darker and more neutral. There is likely to be some change in the hue as well. This is true because black and white pigments both have a cool effect in mixture. There is a resulting shift toward the adjacent cool hue. This effect is particularly noticeable when we mix yellow and black. The black acts as a blue. It lowers both value and intensity and changes the hue toward green. The quality of these greens is quite distinctive. This is a concrete example of the way our approach through the nature of pigment gives a sounder foundation for controlling color than color theory can.

See Plate I, 2a
page 87.

2. When two hue pigments of contrasting value are mixed, the most striking change is in the hue dimension. This is what we normally think about in making such mixtures. At the same time, we shall get a change in value, and, very probably, a change of intensity as well. We have to be aware of these facts to call our shots. Suppose, for example, we want to make a dark yellow. Black will change the hue. We could add a little of the pigment complement of green (red) to compensate for this. A simpler way would be to mix in some raw umber (which is a low value, neutral yellow) instead of black. So hue mixture can be used to control value as well as hue. Even when hue control is our guide, the value changes are important factors.

See Plate I, 4
page 87.

See Plate I, 2b, 2c
page 87.

We are all familiar with the general behavior of pigments mixed to control hue. The principle on which this behavior rests is called *subtractive mixing*. It is explained in the diagram. Pigments act this way because they all reflect a group of related wave lengths of light. We meet monochromatic colors only in the spectrum or under special laboratory conditions. In other words, the color we see in pigments is actually a composite sensation. Wilhelm Ostwald, in his book, *Color Science,** applies the term *semi-chrome* to these groups of related wave lengths. It is a very useful concept for understanding why subtractive mixing works the way it does. When we mix two pigments with different semi-chromes, the reflecting power of the mixture is strongest in those wave lengths that are common to both semi-chromes. Some of the other wave lengths cancel each other. The result is a new semi-chrome that we perceive as a new hue.

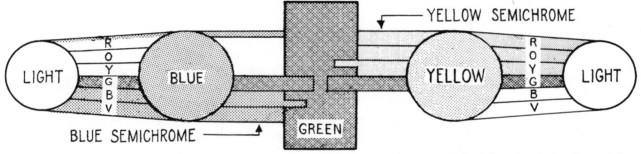

Principle of subtractive mixing.

Some pigments have semi-chromes that are fairly consonant with each other. When we mix them, the new semi-chromes are relatively intense hues. Most red, yellow, and blue pigments, for instance, have more consonant semi-chromes than oranges, greens, and violets. Because of this fact, red, yellow, and blue are often called *primaries*. Orange, green, and violet are called *secondaries*, and the intervening mixtures, *tertiaries*. The underlying consonance and dissonance in the semi-chromes are more important than any theoretical construction of a color circle. What we need is, first, concrete experience with the behavior of pigments in subtractive mixing, and then more experience. We can use as handy rule-of-thumb guides the empirical facts that adjacent hues in the color circuit have a maximum semi-chrome consonance and that red, yellow, and blue is the most consonant triad interval. For real control, we need experience of the infinite range of subtle variation

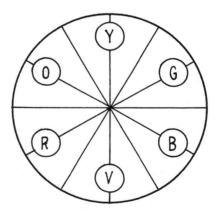

*Wilhelm Ostwald, *Color Science*, Winsor & Newton, Ltd., London, 1933.

69

actual pigments give us. Consider one specific example. On general principles, we expect to get a green when we mix yellow and blue. The actual yellow pigment and the actual blue pigment we use make a great difference in the result, however. Make the experiment yourselves by exploring the sixteen different combinations using four yellows and four blues. Try cadmium yellow light, cadmium medium, yellow ochre, and raw sienna with cobalt blue, ultramarine, cerulean, and phthalocyanine blue. If you do not have these pigments, use as many different yellows and blues as are available. All the mixtures are green—not one green, but sixteen. This shows dramatically how important our point is. In theory, we have one mixed tone. In practice, we have sixteen. Notice also that these sixteen greens vary not only in hue, but in intensity and value. We cannot abstract hue control except in principle. Practically, it is the composite effect that is important.

Controlling Intensity

We defined intensity as the degree of purity in the hue sensation a given tone gives us. We can visualize this dimension as the range between a sensation of maximum hue purity and one in which the same hue has been diluted with achromatic sensation to the point of being just distinguishable from a straight neutral gray.

Every pigment has an intrinsic intensity as well as an intrinsic value level. In some—the cadmium and phthalocyanine colors, for instance—it is very high. The earth colors, on the other hand, come at a more reduced intensity level. Most hues are available in pigments with different intrinsic intensities. This is important to us as designers. It means that we can select the specific pigment that will best serve our purpose. For this reason, we should become familiar with a fairly extensive palette of sound colors whose characteristics we know intimately. Information on reliable pigments may be found in Mayer's *The Artist's Handbook*, and Fischer's *The Permanent Palette*.*

There are four ways of controlling intensity. Three are accomplished by adding to the hue pigment a neutral, black, white, or gray. The fourth way is the addition of the complementary pigment. Each of these methods has distinctive characteristics. Let us examine them in turn.

It will help to visualize these differences if we make use of a modification of Ostwald's color equation. He uses it for quantitative definition. We can adapt it to symbolize the qualitative charac-

* Ralph Mayer, *The Artist's Handbook*, The Viking Press, Inc., New York, 1941. Martin Fischer, *The Permanent Palette*, National Publishing Society, 1930.

70

teristics of our four methods. Any tone can be thought of as a unity composed of three elements in different combinations and proportions. Shorthand for this is $T = H + B + W$. Decoded, this means "tone equals hue plus black plus white."

1. Our first method of controlling intensity is written $T = H + W$, tone equals hue plus white. The resulting tonal range rises in value and diminishes in intensity. The distinctive quality of these tones is perceived as a kind of purity. As a group, they are often called *tints*. Objectively, each one represents the maximum intensity of that pigment at its respective value level.

See Plate I, 3 page 87.

2. The second possibility is represented by the formula $T = H + B$, tone equals hue plus black. This series diminishes in intensity and lowers in value. It also has a distinctive quality as a group, a vibrancy that is quite different from tones controlled by any other means. These tones are often called *shades*. Objectively they, too, represent the maximum intensities of a given pigment at their respective value levels.

3. The third group of tones has the formula $T = H + (B + W)$, tone equals hue plus gray. If the value of the gray is the same as that of the hue pigment, mixtures will give a series of tones varying only in *intensity*. If the gray is lighter or darker, the change will be in both intensity and value. The word *tones* is sometimes applied to this group. Since we are using *tone* to designate the whole range of chromatic and achromatic color qualities, *grayed tones* will be more descriptive. The presence of gray in them is very evident and gives them quite a different quality from our tints and shades in spite of the fact that a given grayed tone and a given tint may have the same relative intensity.

4. The final method of controlling intensity is represented by the formula $T = H + cH$, tone equals hue plus its complement. When the semi-chromes of two pigments stand in clear opposition, their mixture will result in a neutral gray. Such pigments are called *complementary*. Examples are ultramarine blue and burnt sienna or cadmium red medium and chromium oxide green. They produce a series of tones ranging through different degrees of intensity to neutral gray. This series has special properties, too. The tones will have to be classed as grayed tones since they bear a close resemblance to our last series. They have a certain liveliness, however, that tones neutralized with gray lack. I suggest that you select some hue pigment from your palette of colors, and explore these four ways of controlling intensity. Make a range of tones with white, with black, with gray, and with the complementary hue. The exact complement may not be represented by any straight pigment. You may have to mix it. A little experimentation will determine the proper

71

balance. Try particularly to see the subtle qualities that characterize your tints, shades, and grayed tones.

These are the fundamental possibilities. We can extend the range up to a point by combining them. For instance, the formula $T = H_1 + H_2 + W$ or B indicates another frequent practice. We usually add black or white in a case of this kind to raise or lower the value of our tone. From what we have said, there is also an effect on the resulting intensity.

The distinctive qualities of tones neutralized by these four methods, that is, with white, with black, with gray, and with a complement, are subtle. They are also very important. When we have developed our color sensitivity to the point where we respond not only to degrees of intensity, but also to the subtle values of harmony and contrast which we can build from these secondary qualities, those values become an expressive resource.

We have considered the methods of controlling the three dimensions of color. Now let us see the significance of these techniques as they affect the range of tones.

THE RANGE OF TONES

When you begin to work with color, you are likely to use pigments pretty much as a child uses his crayons. You color one area blue, the next yellow, another red, and so on till your colors are all used up. That is an extreme statement, of course, but I am willing to bet that most of you are familiar with the feeling of running out of colors. Such an experience is always due to the fact that you do not appreciate the resources in the three dimensions of your tones. They are practically inexhaustible, even in a very restricted palette.

The only way to realize the potential richness of tonal range which the three color dimensions give us is through experience. Practice and more practice with color is the best training. But this practice needs to be guided by a critical awareness of what we are doing. Otherwise the experience lacks articulation. We shall still be depending on chance effect, rather than developing usable control of the material.

Values and Intensities of One Hue

We shall outline the basic possibilities to serve us as guides in our study. Take first the range of tone we can get out of one hue pig-

72

ment with black and white. We can represent this range as a triangle with the hue at the apex and the neutral scale from white to black as the base. One leg, from hue to white, represents the varying values and intensities we can get by mixing these two pigments. The other, from hue to black, represents that sequence. Within the triangle lie all tones in which all three pigments are used. The actual number of tones we can get out of these mixtures will depend on the hue pigment itself. Different pigments vary greatly in their tinting power. Some, like terre-verte, are very weak. Their hue quality is swallowed, as it were, in mixture with black and white. Such pigments will give us only a small triangle of mixed tones. Other pigments, such as phthalocyanine green (to stick to the same hue), have a very high tinting power. With them we can make greatly extended ranges of tones by adding only black and white, and it would take a much larger triangle to show the organization of all these tones.

Now we shall consider the characteristic patterns we get by mixing between two hue pigments. The interval between the tones selected will affect the consonance of their semi-chromes. On this depends the behavior of the mixtures.

*See Plate I, 3
page 87.*

Analogous Hue Interval

When the hue step between the pigments is small, as between cadmium yellow pale and phthalocyanine green, there will be a high degree of consonance in the semi-chromes. The mixed tones will vary in hue through various yellow-greens. There will be little loss of intensity through canceling out of conflicting wave lengths. The value will fall between the value levels of the pigments mixed. Where we want high intensity in mixed tones, this is the best procedure. For this reason, it is a good practice to include several reds, yellows, and blues in your palette. In the mixture we are discussing, a cadmium yellow pale is a better choice to give intense yellow-greens than a cadmium yellow medium. The latter is closer to orange in its hue. This makes a wider interval with less consonance between the semi-chromes. The resulting mixtures are consequently more neutralized because of the presence of red wave lengths in the yellow semi-chrome. On the other hand, the reduction in intensity and greater warmth of the mixed tone that results is sometimes just what we want. These subtle differences in behavior of mixtures are what we need to know in order to choose our pigments effectively.

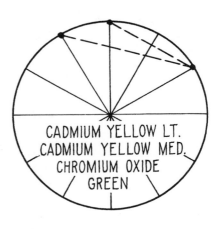

CADMIUM YELLOW LT.
CADMIUM YELLOW MED.
CHROMIUM OXIDE
GREEN

*See Plate II, 1a, 1b
page 90.*

73

Triad Hue Interval

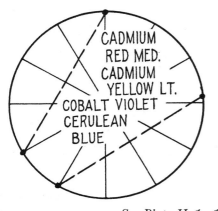

CADMIUM
RED MED.
CADMIUM
YELLOW LT.
COBALT VIOLET
CERULEAN
BLUE

See Plate II, 1c, 1d page 90.

The *triad interval* offers a second characteristic pattern. There is no reason, of course, why we cannot use a somewhat lesser or greater step. If we understand how the median interval behaves, we shall know what to expect from the variations. We have to distinguish between primary intervals and other triads. It so happens that our red, yellow, and blue pigments have more nearly consonant semi-chromes than other triad combinations. Consequently, mixture between two primaries will give us more intense intermediate tones than secondary or tertiary mixtures. Nevertheless, the general pattern is the same. We shall have a wider hue range than we can get out of analogous tones, but there will be a greater loss of intensity. This is particularly true with secondaries and tertiaries. There may also be a wider value interval between the two tones with a greater value range in the mixtures.

Complementary Hue Interval

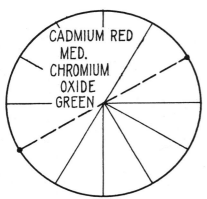

CADMIUM RED
MED.
CHROMIUM
OXIDE
GREEN

See Plate II, 1e page 90.

The third characteristic pattern is found in *complementary mixtures*. Here the semi-chromes are directly opposed. An optically balanced mixture will reflect equal quantities of all wave lengths, and absorb an equal portion of them all. The result is a neutral gray of intermediate value. In unequal mixtures, one or the other hue will dominate, giving, as we have seen, a range of intensities for that hue. If the complements are of the same value, there will be little value change in the series. This is approximately true of cadmium red medium and chromium oxide green. Most complementary pigments contrast in value. The mixtures between them will vary in value as well as in intensity.

Remember that each tone in these patterns can be mixed also with white, black, and gray, giving a further value and intensity range. The illustration shows how this works for two tones selected from the previous patterns.

Range of Tones for Three Pigments

Finally, consider what happens when we mix three hue pigments. We can select any set of interval relationships between these tones. If the steps are equal, we shall have a straight triad pattern. When we select unequal intervals, many combinations are possible, all variations on the basic intervals. We normally make such selections on the basis of hue qualities. It is important, though, to analyze the intervals involved. If we have a clear picture of these, it helps enormously to visualize the tonal possibilities we can get out of the combination. We shall analyze one. It is representative of the behavior of all.

Take cadmium red light (approximately a red-orange), yellow ochre (a yellow-orange of lesser intensity), and ultramarine blue (a slightly violet blue). The cadmium and the yellow ochre are related by an analogous step. The ochre and the ultramarine are almost complementary. The cadmium and ultramarine are separated by a little more than a triad step.

*See Plate I, 4
page 87.*

Mixture between each pair of tones will give us the same sort of patterns as are analyzed above. Mixtures in which varying proportions of all three tones are used will yield a range of more neutralized tones including a wide variety of toned grays and browns. Every one of these tones can also be mixed with black, white, or gray. If you digest these resources, you need never run out of colors again!

In Chapter 8, we shall consider the possibilities for using the intrinsic relationships of such limited palettes to get color harmony in our compositions. For the time being, we are interested in the wide range of potential tones they contain. We can go on, adding four, five, six, and more hue pigments to the limits of available colors. The analysis of the resulting tonal ranges will repeat the same essential pattern we have just considered. Particularly at the beginning, though, it is much better to limit your exploration to groups of three hues and black and white. This gives you a wide enough range for interest and variety. At the same time, the relationships are simple enough to be clearly understood. Practice of this kind, and the application of these tonal ranges to simple problems of painting, layout, pattern designing, and so on, will give you invaluable experience. You will build up a working knowledge of pigment and how to control it. At the same time, you will be sharpening your sensitivity to tonal qualities and their relationships. This integrated experience is the foundation for all the other problems of color organization.

READING LIST

Fischer, Martin: *The Permanent Palette*, National Publishing Society, 1930.

International Printing Ink: *Three Monographs on Color*, International Printing Ink Corp., 1935.

Mayer, Ralph: *The Artist's Handbook*, The Viking Press, Inc., New York, 1941.

Sargent, Walter: *The Enjoyment and Use of Color*, Charles Scribner's Sons, New York, 1923. Chapters 2 and 4.

PROBLEM V

Purpose:

To explore the problems of controlling pigment tones.

Problems:

1. Exploring a limited palette.
   - *a.* Select three hue pigments and black and white. Any three hues will serve, but I suggest that you do not pick a straight primary triad. Since you are probably most familiar with its behavior, a different combination will be more revealing.
   - *b.* Begin with the single hues. Paint swatches about 4 inches square. Make one at the natural value and intensity level of the pigment. Then make several mixtures with white and several with black to give a range of value and intensity.
   - *c.* Next, make mixtures between pairs of hues. Make a fairly extended range of tones, varying the proportions of the colors. For every other tone, say, make some lighter and darker values using white and black.
   - *d.* Finally, make mixtures in which you use varying proportions of all three hues. Lighter and darker values of some of these tones should be made.

You should end with at least a hundred different tones. If you do this systematically, observing carefully the behavior of your mixtures, you can learn a great deal about the behavior of your selected palette. I do not advise trying to label each mixture. This makes the process too mechanical. Rather, try to get the feel of how the pigments work.

2. On a sheet of illustration board, lay out twenty-four 4-inch squares, allowing margin around each one. Now, with scissors and paste, make a different color pattern in each. Include the following:
   - *a.* Make some patterns on white grounds.
   - *b.* Some with colored grounds.
   - *c.* Some with black and some with gray grounds.
   - *d.* Use a divided ground of two tones in one or two.

You will find the best way of proceeding is to select your ground tone, then to pick two or three tones to use with it. Do not draw a set pattern ahead of time, but add shapes and tones as each composition requires. Do not try to make pictures. Let the whole response be to the tone relationships.

Specifications:

1. Materials:
   - *a.* Use any inexpensive paper that will take water color without too much wrinkling.
   - *b.* Work in opaque water color or poster paint. There is no harm in having texture in some of your swatches.
2. Presentation:
   - *a.* Title the sheet "Limited Palette."
   - *b.* Include small swatches of the three hues on which the range is based, labeled with the pigment name.
   - *c.* Great care must be taken in pasting not to smear the surface of your tones. Be neat and craftsmanlike.

I recommend that you explore a wide range of pigments as in 2, 3, and 4 above. Make small swatches of each tone (about 2 by 2 inches). Cut them out and store them in a cigar box. You will find that an excellent way to get color ideas, whenever the need arises, is to get them out and play with them.

7 THE DYNAMICS OF COLOR

We have to think of the problem of controlling our tones at two levels. In the last chapter we were concerned with the first of these, the production of a given tone out of our pigment resources. But we rarely use colors alone. In the great majority of cases, we use them in combination. The problem of their relationship, as we shall now see, is a second major factor in controlling our desired effect.

We can state this as an axiom. *To know what a tone will look like, we must know not only what it is in itself, but where it is in its environment.* This is what I mean by the term *color dynamics*. There is a complete relativity between the tones in a composition. The contrasts between them affect perception. This influence is so strong at times that the apparent nature of a tone on the palette is completely changed in context. The psychologists call this effect *simultaneous contrast*. Let us see how it works.

HOW SIMULTANEOUS CONTRAST AFFECTS TONES

The basic principle is simple. Whenever two different tones come into direct contact, the contrast will intensify the differences between them. This change will be greater in proportion to the degree of contrast, both in the tonal dimensions and in the area of contact. That means that two colors that are similar in value, hue, and intensity will not have much effect on each other. Where the contrast in these dimensions, singly or in combination, is strong, we can expect a marked change. It also means that the more one tone comes into contact with another, the greater the change will be. The maximum condition will be when one tone is surrounded by another.

See Plate III, 1
page 91.

The effect of simultaneous contrast is reciprocal. Both tones are affected. We are usually more conscious of it in the figure element. You can see that this is true from the illustrations. What you notice is that the circle spots of identical pigment look different on different grounds. You have a basis of comparison so that the differences show up clearly. There is no standard of comparison to make you aware of changes in the ground. Nevertheless, all the tones in a composition are influenced by the tones with which they come into contact. Once you are aware of this fact, you will become very conscious of reciprocal action as you work with color. If you are painting a picture, for instance, you will mix the tone you think you want. Then you will have to take a bit on the palette knife and hold it up to the tones it is going to touch in the picture. Usually you find that adjustments have to be made. It will look lighter or darker, warmer or cooler, more or less intense than you intended. If you understand how this relativity works, you are much better equipped to control your tones. What we shall do, then, is to consider each type of contrast in turn. This is the only way to understand the problem. At the same time, it is arbitrary. In practice, you will have to deal with patterns of change in which all the tonal dimensions are involved.

Value Contrast

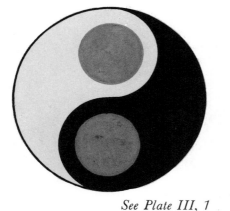

See Plate III, 1
page 91.

When two different values are presented in simultaneous contrast, the lighter one will look lighter, the darker one darker. This effect is very obvious when we take a middle gray and put it on a white ground and a black ground respectively. In one case, the gray is objectively darker than the ground; in the other, objectively lighter. On the white ground, it will look much darker than it does on the black.

While this is the most extreme case, the same thing will happen wherever the values of two adjacent tones differ. Remember that the ground tone is affected as well as the figure tone. This works just as positively for chromatic tones as for neutrals. The effect may be more complex because the other tone dimensions will probably be involved too.

Hue Contrast

The effect is a little more complicated when we contrast different hues. This is because the differences between hues are qualitative. (Value differences are only quantitative.) The change will be

78

toward a different hue. The guiding principle here is temperature contrast. When a warmer tone is presented in simultaneous contrast with a cooler one, the warm tone will look warmer, the cool tone cooler. More specifically, there will be a shift in the apparent hue toward the adjacent warmer or cooler hue. In the illustration, for instance, the same green tone has been put on a yellow ground and a blue ground. On the yellow it is relatively cool. On the blue it is relatively warm. The green appears, in the first case, much greener than it is; in the second, it appears much yellower.

See Plate III, 1 page 91.

A similar thing happens when we contrast a hue and a neutral tone. The psychological complement of the hue will be induced in the neutral. Thus, a gray spot on a blue ground will look yellowish; on a yellow ground, bluish, and so forth. This effect is most positive under two conditions, when the hue is high in intensity and when the gray is above middle value. The circle spots in the illustration demonstrate this effect. The same idea is often exploited in painting. The delicate Delft blue tiles in Dutch seventeenth-century interiors by De Hooch, Ter Borch, and Vermeer were painted with black and white pigment. The blue tonality is induced by the surrounding colors. The fragile pinks in Monet's water lily series are grays toned by the misty blues and greens that surround them.

Intensity Contrast

There are two sorts of relativity changes in the intensity dimension. Both illustrate the intensification of opposites, but in different ways. First, take contrasts between analogous hues of different intensities. The simple law of increased difference applies. The objectively more intense tone looks more intense than it is; the objectively less intense tone looks more neutral than it is. This simple opposition is complicated when complementary and near-complementary hues are contrasted. Since each induces its complement, the effect is to increase the apparent intensity of both tones. This effect is of maximum strength when the tones are high in intensity. It can become so powerful that the contrast is physically painful to look at. Take the red-orange spot on the green-blue ground. These tones are approximately complementary. Both are full intensity. The apparent intensity of each is greater than the same tone on a white ground. The conflict between them is too strong for comfort. To use such contrasts successfully, we must do one or more of three things. We must subordinate the area of one tone drastically so that the other dominates; we must reduce the intensity of one tone to subordinate it; or we must isolate the two tones with a neutral, thereby weakening the simultaneous contrast. This sort of intensification of both tones

See Plate III, 1 page 91.

holds even when the hues are neutralized, but it is more restrained.

To sum up, there are five kinds of contrast effects to distinguish. Two of them, value contrasts and intensity contrasts between the same or analogous hues, result in the simple accenting of differences. Hue contrast acts to increase the temperature contrast between the tones, causing an apparent shift in hue. Chromatic-achromatic contrast tends to cause complementary induction in the neutral tone. Complementary hue contrast causes an increased apparent intensity in both tones.

This strong relativity of tones in combination has important consequences in the technique of using color. The painter, for instance, has a special problem. The areas he lays in first are judged against an entirely different ground from the one they will have in the finished picture. As he builds up his tones and contrasts, the balance is continually changing. This means that he has to develop the ability to visualize the ultimate effect of his colors and to try to establish not what looks right at the moment, but what will look right when the relativity is established. If you have ever tried painting water-color landscapes, I am sure you have had the experience of laying in a sky at the beginning only to find the tone completely washed out when you got on with the composition. You have to learn to lay it in much darker than you want it. The point is that by contrast with the white paper, the tone will seem much darker. When the actual contrasting tones have been established, it will necessarily appear lighter.

A number of techniques have been developed to help the painter solve this difficulty. This is not a book on painting, but as an illustration of this point it is worth while to discuss them here. One way around the difficulty has been to lay in the composition in neutral tones, establishing the whole value pattern. You usually keep it several steps lighter than you want the finished picture. Over this you either glaze in your colors, or sometimes paint the whole thing in body color, completely covering the underpainting. This is not the only purpose in using the method, but it has the effect of simplifying the relativity problem. You have to worry only about value relativity in the underpainting. That pattern being set, the overpainting can concentrate on hue and intensity relations. Another method is to lay in a quick stain of color thinned in turpentine for each color area. This is a first approximation of your tone relationships and serves to give you a much closer basis for judging the final tones. One other frequently used method is to cover the whole canvas with a flat wash approximating the tonality you want in the finished picture. This again gives you a much more accurate basis for judging the effect of your tones as you lay them in. From this behavior of simultaneous contrast two other basic practices in painting follow: You can judge the gradually developing relationships much better if you work the whole canvas at once. This means adding an area here, another there so that the whole composition advances at about the same rate. The other practice is the negative side of what we have just said. It is dangerous to finish up one part of the composition before surrounding parts have been established. This is an almost universal failing with beginners. It has to be guarded against vigorously.

All these practices stem largely from the one fact that you have to know where your color is in its environment, as well as what it is, to know how it is going to look. The same thing is true for any use of color in relationship. If you are interested in layout design or interior design or architecture or ceramics or textiles or whatever, you have to master the mechanics of color relativity before you can make color do what you want it to. This is another and very cogent reason why color theory, which treats these problems in the abstract, is a less serviceable guide than we would like.

THE EFFECT OF TONE CONTRAST ON FORM

There is another aspect to the problem of color dynamics. Tone and contrast affect not only the apparent dimensions of our colors; they affect the form of their areas as well.

Let us examine a number of the more significant ways in which tone contrast affects form.

Spreading of Light Values

We have already seen that a light color on a dark ground looks lighter than it really is, a dark color on a light ground darker. We now discover that the light tone seems larger in area, the dark smaller. You have doubtless been conscious of this in looking at a light source against a dark ground. The light seems to spread. The edges have streamers that penetrate into the surrounding dark. The same thing happens in a less violent way with light and dark tone contrasts. The light spot irradiates the ground, seeming to increase in size. The light ground irradiates the dark spot, making it seem to shrink.

A homely application of this dynamism is the common rule that stout women should wear dark colors. For maximum effectiveness, they should carry the application one step farther. They should be careful always to let themselves be seen in silhouette against a light background!

81

Temperature Contrast

See Plate III, 3 page 91.

A similar dynamic effect is present when we contrast warm and cool tones. The warm tone appears larger, the cool smaller, than it actually is. When this effect is co-ordinated with the spreading of lights (for instance, a warm light tone against a cool dark ground), the illusion is striking.

There is a second dynamic effect of temperature and temperature contrasts. This has both a physiological and a psychological foundation. Different wave lengths of light require different adjustments in the curvature of our optical lenses to focus the image on the retina. The principle is clear if we think of what happens when light passes through a prism. Because of the difference in wave length, the colors are deflected to varying degrees. The result is the spreading out of the wave lengths into the familiar spectrum. Red, the longest wave length, is deflected least. Blue-violet, the shortest wave length, is deflected most. The other wave lengths distribute themselves between in regular order. A lens of given curvature, therefore, cannot be equally accurate in focusing all wave lengths. This shows up in the science of optics. It is responsible for the effect of *chromatic aberration* around the edges of simple lenses. In precision cameras and optical instruments elaborate compound lenses have to be designed to overcome this difficulty.

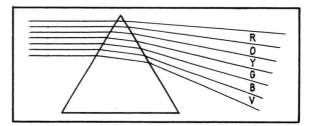

Diffraction of long and short wave lengths.

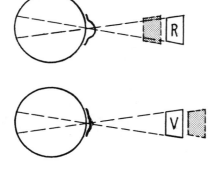

Visual adaptation to long and short wave lengths.

Our eyes solve the problem in a simple but marvelous way. The curvature of the lens itself changes. So the lenses thicken in focusing red, and thin out in focusing blue-violet. Other tones have their intermediate adjustments. Now notice that this pattern exactly parallels the action of the lens in focusing near and far objects, although the adjustment is much less pronounced. Here is the physiological basis for the advancing and receding qualities of warm and cool tones.

These qualities are enhanced by our associations with colors. Warm tones have a connotation of fire and heat, expansion, opening out. Cool tones remind us of ice, water, deep sky.

82

The dual effect of these psychological and physiological factors influences our perception of tones. Warm tones seem to advance and expand; cool tones, to recede and contract. These qualities are particularly powerful when temperature contrasts are involved. Look at the red-orange circle on the green-blue ground again. Not only does complementary intensification result, but the two tones require quite different adaptation in our optic lenses as well. If you fixate the edge, where contrast is greatest, you can feel the strain. As you look, the edge takes on thickness. A brighter line of color appears on both sides. The red spot has almost a stereopticon effect. It does not seem to lie on the ground, but in front of it. It is interesting to reverse the relationship. Look at the green-blue spot on the red-orange ground. See how the ground comes forward. The figure makes a hole in it.

See Plate III, 1
page 91.

These temperature effects of color are very important in composition. They have a direct application, for instance, to interior design. We can increase the effect of space in a small room by using cool, receding tones. We can make a large room more intimate by using warm, advancing tones. We can improve disproportionately long or narrow spaces by the optical illusion of pushing out the side walls with cool tones and bringing in the end walls with warm ones.

These advancing and receding activities of color are equally significant in two-dimensional compositions. Correlated with the natural effects of light, they are essential to an understanding of atmospheric perspective. In their own right they can be used to indicate space and volume. We shall consider these space-building possibilities of temperature contrast for two-dimensional organization more in detail later on.

Color Weight

A third factor in the effect of tone on form is that tones change the apparent weight or specific gravity of the forms to which they are applied. Cool and light tones appear lighter and less substantial. Warm and dark tones appear heavier and denser. Applying this to three-dimensional forms, we can modify the apparent actual weight of an object. During the war, I worked for a while as an aircraft sheet-metal mechanic. It was interesting to see the difference in expression between the planes that were finished in the natural silver of their duralumin skins and those that had been painted lead gray or olive drab for combat. As you watched them take off on the line, you had the feeling that the latter worked much harder to get into the air. This effect of weight is also apparent in two-dimensional forms. It has a great deal to do with the expressive use of color.

TONE CONTRAST AND COMPOSITION

The final point in our discussion of the effect of tone on form is how the kind and distribution of tone contrasts work in the composition. That tone attraction and contrast attraction are important compositional factors is evident from our discussions in Chapters 4 and 5. I have in mind here another aspect of the problem that we have only touched on before. This will be most easily presented through the illustrations. I have taken two patterns identical in form and developed both with the same four values. I have tried to keep the relative proportion of the tones similar in both patterns. By distributing the tones in different areas, a quite different compositional form develops in each design. The patterns of movement, balance, and rhythm are changed, as we would expect. The particular factor I want to demonstrate, though, is the modification of the figure-ground and pattern organizations. Each tone acquires certain values as figure or ground. When these tones are distributed in different areas, the whole formal structure of the design changes. On the basis of these relationships, we put the pattern together in different ways.

In a sense the demonstration is a trick. We would not be likely to make this sort of controlled contrast very often. The point is that our tones behave in this way in any composition. We may not make a point of it by contrast as we have here. Nevertheless, the way in which we distribute our tones is as important as the shapes and areas we give them in determining our composition.

In organizing a visual field, tone and tone relations serve a dual function. First, we have seen that tone contrasts are the visual raw materials with which we work as designers. Second, their intrinsic dynamism and attractions act with the shapes, sizes, and positions of the elements to create the composition. We have two methods of building the desired relationship between the forms and tones in our pattern. Sometimes we start with a set form. We draw the shapes and areas abstracted from their color. Then we build in the tone pattern. Since form is set, every tone and contrast has to be adjusted exactly to its place and function in the composition. This method is often forced upon us. In architecture, interior design, products design, layout, and so on, the form has to meet exact functional requirements. We have to fit the form to the function and the color to the form. Not that we make quite such a bald separation as this suggests. We always have color in mind as we are working out our forms. Still the adjustment has to be made in our tonal dimensions to make our pattern work.

The other possibility is to develop the shapes, sizes, and positions of our areas with their tone qualities all at the same time. This is both a more flexible and a more complex process. It is also more organic in that tone and area are never divorced. It is especially the method of painting. Undeniably, much great painting has resulted from the first method—starting with a cartoon and working on into color. Nevertheless, the ideal is to build directly in pigment, letting the form develop out of the color.

Both ways of working are excellent training in color dynamics. They complement each other. They are equally important technical resources. Some problems can best be handled one way, some the other. You should be competent to solve the problem of color-form relationship in either way, whichever fits your purpose better.

READING LIST

International Printing Ink: *Three Monographs on Color*, International Printing Ink Corp., New York, 1935.

Sargent, Walter: *The Enjoyment and Use of Color*, Charles Scribner's Sons, New York, 1923. Chapter 3.

PROBLEM VI

Purpose:

    1. To explore the basic principles of tone relativity.
    2. To experiment with the effect of tone on composition.

Problems:

    1. You can work out this problem best by experimenting first with the color swatches left from the previous problem. When you have your solutions, it will be good practice to mix new tones to match those you want to use. Make four pairs of color patterns 4 inches square as follows:

        a. One pair in which one figure tone common to both patterns is made to appear different in value. (Use identical patterns in both compositions so that the change will be clear.) You will do this by changing the ground tone. Two tones are sufficient, but you can increase the effect by a careful choice of additional tones. For instance, if your control tone is a middle-value gray and you want it to appear lighter, you will select a dark ground. If the ground for the gray is placed on a light tone, it will itself seem darker, thus enhancing its effect on the gray figure.

        b. One pair in which one figure tone common to both patterns is made to appear different in hue. You may use either a neutral or a hue tone for the control tone.

        c. One pair in which one figure tone common to both patterns is made to appear different in intensity. It is difficult to restrict the changes to a single color dimension. It will be good practice for you to try to do this as clearly as possible. In any event, put the emphasis definitely on the dimension in question.

        d. One pair in which one figure tone common to both patterns is made to appear different in value, hue, and intensity.

    2. Draw two identical patterns in 8- by 10-inch formats. Develop these on the basis of the whole to the parts, as in Problem IV, page 66. Develop the patterns in color as follows:

        a. Restrict your tones to four or five, as necessary for your particular pattern.

        b. Change the position of your tones from one pattern to the next. Try to keep the total amount of each tone approximately the same in both patterns. (Make sure you use the same areas in both patterns. Do not paint two adjacent areas the same tone.)

        c. Try to make both patterns equally effective compositions.

Specifications:

    1. Materials:
    Use a sheet of illustration board and poster paint or opaque water color.

    2. Presentation:

        a. Lay out your areas on the board, allowing space for titling. Paint your designs directly on the board.

        b. Title the sheet "Color Relativity." Title each pair of patterns to explain its significance.

PLATE I

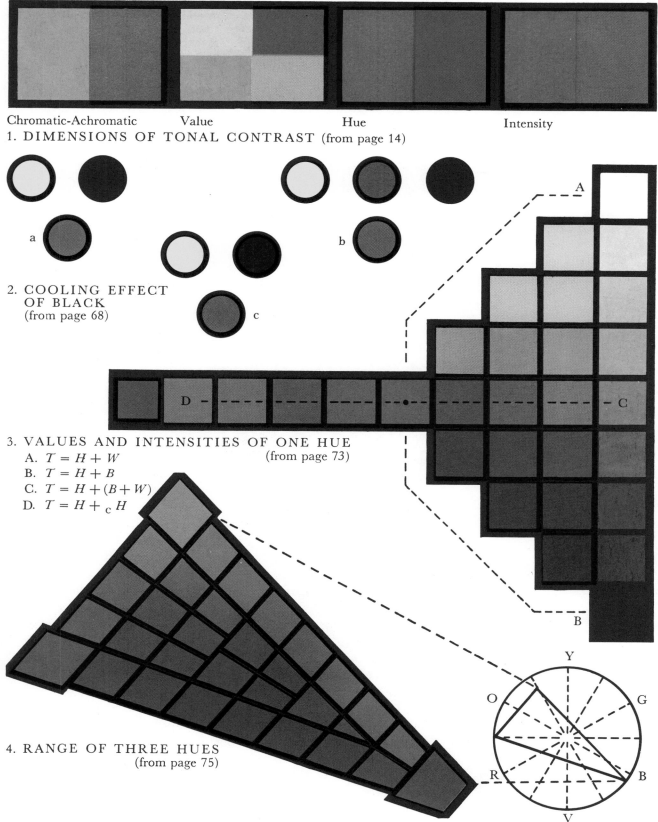

Chromatic-Achromatic   Value   Hue   Intensity

1. DIMENSIONS OF TONAL CONTRAST (from page 14)

a   b

2. COOLING EFFECT
   OF BLACK
   (from page 68)

c

3. VALUES AND INTENSITIES OF ONE HUE (from page 73)

   A. $T = H + W$
   B. $T = H + B$
   C. $T = H + (B + W)$
   D. $T = H + {}_c H$

4. RANGE OF THREE HUES
   (from page 75)

8 COLOR RELATIONSHIPS

To tell what a tone will look like we have to know what it is in itself and where it is in relation to other tones. We have studied each of these factors in the preceding chapters. Now we are ready to take up the question of the pattern of relationships in a color composition.

We can state this problem very simply. It is the same as that of composition generally, variety in unity. What we have to do is to find out how to create unity between our tones and how to keep that unity alive and interesting with variety.

This is not a problem that can be solved by the application of set rules. With color, more than with any other design factor, your feeling for harmony is the final guiding principle. It is true that rule and system can insure you against positively bad color. They cannot guarantee distinguished color. This is true because both color perception and our reactions to color relationships are such subjective processes.

At the same time, handling color is a highly technical problem. You cannot expect to buy a paintbox and proceed to create masterpieces overnight. Your intrinsic feeling for color can express itself only to the degree to which you have developed technical control over your tones. That feeling itself is largely potential at the beginning. You have to develop and refine it through experience. One of the exciting things about designing is that this growth can go on maturing throughout a lifetime. There is never a point at which you can say it is complete.

We all have this feeling for color to a greater or less degree. An exercise such as I recommended at the end of Chapter 6 is proof of this. I have observed it over and over in my classes. Let the student assemble tones by trial and error without committing himself by tying them down to a given shape, size, and position until he is satisfied. He will invariably produce color organizations far beyond his abilities to paint directly. This is because we can judge relationships when we see them much more sensitively than we can visualize them, at least until we have built up a rich background of experience. Our color problem, therefore, is double. We have to develop dependable technical control, and we have to refine and sharpen our natural sensitivity.

Some order in the problems of relationship is as great a help in refining sensitivity as in developing control. This is the real value of color system. It helps us to direct our attention to the significant things. It makes us aware of what our reactions and evaluations are based on.

Now, let us see what foundation there is in our perceptions themselves for achieving such order.

PHYSIOLOGICAL-PSYCHOLOGICAL BASIS FOR COLOR RELATIONS

Likeness

In Chapter 3, we considered likeness in the tonal dimensions as a basis for figure grouping. The mere fact that we can see an element of sameness between tones is one factor that ties them together. It is one of the roots of color unity. We can express this sameness in any one of the tonal dimensions—value, hue, and intensity—or in a combination of them. The more complex tonal structure of temperature qualities and chromatic-achromatic grouping gives us two more fundamental similarities. The simplest application of this fact of recognition based on likeness is straight repetition. Look at any color organization you consider effective. Almost invariably you will find the same tones repeated in different parts of the composition. Simple as this device is, it provides one of the soundest methods of unifying our color organizations. The same value of recognition arises if closely related rather than identical tones are repeated. Here the element of change introduces both variety and the opportunity for subtle ties in the patterns of color relations.

PLATE II

Cadmium Yellow Pale

Cadmium Y. Medium

Chromium Oxide Green

B A

C

E

Cadmium Red. Med.

Viridian Deep

D

Cobalt Violet

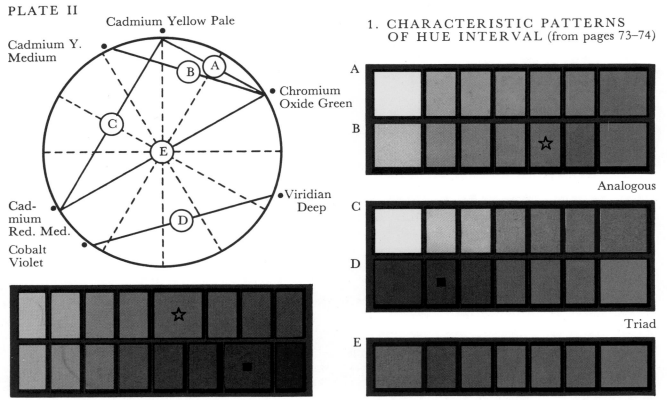

1. CHARACTERISTIC PATTERNS OF HUE INTERVAL (from pages 73–74)

A

B

Analogous

C

D

Triad

E

Complementary

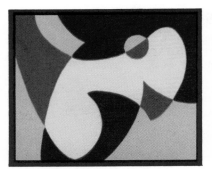

Extended Value and Intensity Ranges

2. HUE KEYS: Characteristic patterns based on equal intervals of hue contrast

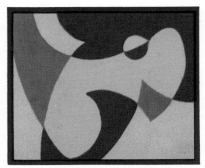

Warm Analogous

Approximate Primary Triad

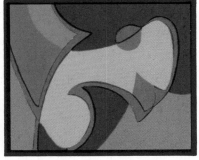

Complementary: High intensity —small area

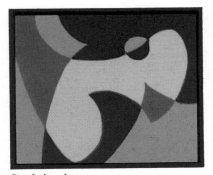

Cool Analogous

Approximate Secondary Triad

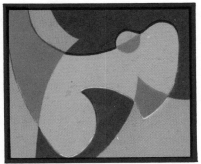

Complementary: Reduced intensity—larger area

90

PLATE III

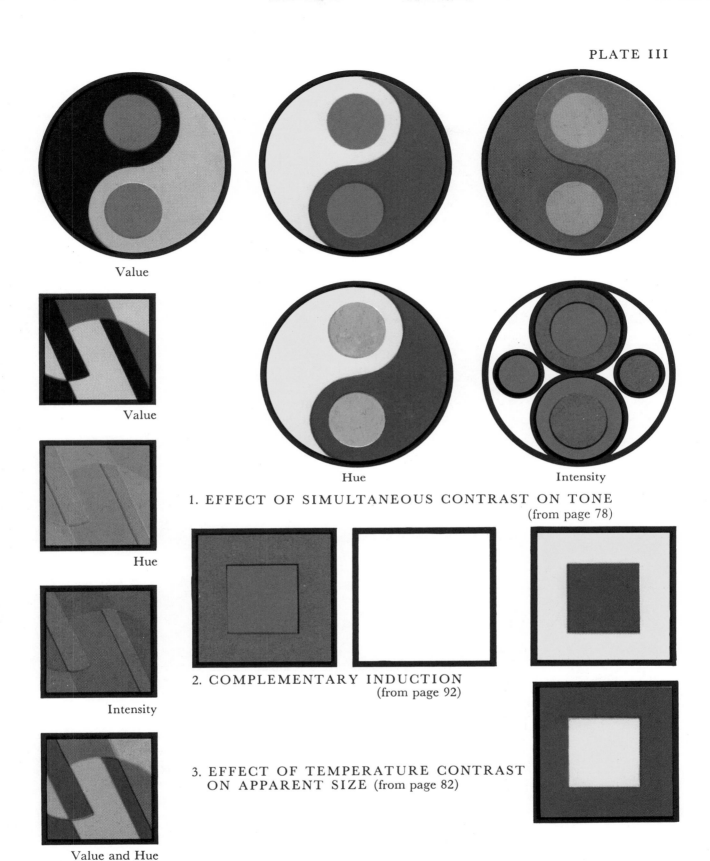

Value

Value

Hue

Intensity

Value and Hue

Hue

Intensity

1. EFFECT OF SIMULTANEOUS CONTRAST ON TONE
(from page 78)

2. COMPLEMENTARY INDUCTION
(from page 92)

3. EFFECT OF TEMPERATURE CONTRAST
ON APPARENT SIZE (from page 82)

4. EFFECT OF CONTRAST IN THE DIFFERENT TONAL DIMENSIONS ON FORM
(from page 93)

The second fact of perception that helps us to organize our tones is *sequence*. We perceive an intrinsic order among hues. The physical basis of this order is the correlation between the sequence of light wave lengths and the hues we see in the spectrum. The order is the same. If we take yellow out of its place between orange and green and put it in after blue, it will upset the sequence. We will feel that it is out of place. But there is another significant fact about the way we perceive this order. The physical sequence of wave lengths is a linear progression from roughly 400 to 700 millimicrons. But we see the same kind of relationship between the two ends of this progression as between the other steps. To diagram what we perceive, we shall have to use a circle instead of a straight line. Remember from Chapter 2 that we actually see some composite hues in this interval between red and violet that are not in the spectrum. They complete the circular sequence. This fact of an intrinsic sequence in our hue perceptions is a most significant root of tonal unity. We shall develop its implications shortly.

The same kind of intrinsic order is apparent in both the value and intensity dimensions. If we transpose any step in the value or intensity ranges, we perceive directly that it is out of place. In other words, there is a given order in our perceptions of the sequence from light to dark and from chromatic to achromatic. Like hue sequence, this order can be made the organizing principle for unity in tone relations.

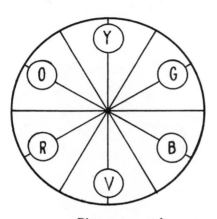

Pigment complements.

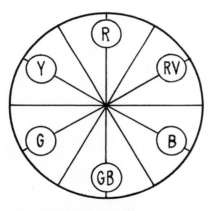

Psychological complements.

See Plate III, 2 page 91.

Psychological Complements

The third important fact of perception is that our color vision determines complementary relationships. I pointed out the distinction between pigment complements and design complements in Chapter 6. The former result from the semi-chrome nature of pigments. The latter are the consequence of our physiological-psychological make-up. If we look fixedly at a spot of intense red, then shift our eyes to a white area, we will see an afterimage of the spot in green-blue, its psychological complement. (See the illustration.) Every tone will behave in a similar way. The major psychological complements are shown in the diagram and contrasted with the approximate pigment complements. This fact gives us another basic relationship between hues. It is rather one of opposition than one of unity; but it is regulated by the same sort of intrinsic law of perception as hue sequence, and is of great importance to tone relations.

Next, we shall explore the implications of these facts.

STRUCTURE OF TONE RELATIONS

The use of simple similarities in any of the tonal dimensions is so obvious that we need spend little time on it. There is just one point to emphasize. We must not forget in our concern for harmonizing our color relationships that the form of our visual pattern depends on contrast. We always have to strike a just balance between the similarities that tie our pattern together and the differences that make it a pattern at all. This is particularly important for the value dimension. Look at the four repeated patterns in the illustration. I have adjusted the tones so that each one emphasizes contrast in different tonal qualities. See how much more positive the form is in the first pattern where value contrast is used. In the second, in spite of a strong hue contrast, the form is weak. In the third, where the intensities alone are different, the form is weakest of all. In the fourth, contrast in both value and hue makes the most positive statement of form.

*See Plate III, 4
page 91.*

We can see from this demonstration that value difference is our most effective single contrast for establishing form. Therefore we must be very careful in harmonizing values not to lose the required degree of contrast necessary to give structure to the design. Such contrast can be dramatic or subtle according to the needs of the composition. Lack of proper contrast, though, is a frequent cause of unsatisfactory color organization. One of the most disagreeable combinations we meet in color patterns is that in which different adjacent forms are the same in value and strongly contrasted in hue. We realize that we are intended to see them as separate forms, but the hue contrast does not hold its own against the tie-up in value. The result is a disagreeable conflict in perception. The reverse side of this picture is equally important. When we have different hues in the same form, either as pattern or broken-color texture, we have to be very careful with the value contrasts. If we make them too strong, we can easily break up a form that should be read as a unit.

Interval Relationships

There is another and more subtle kind of similarity we can use to knit our tones together. This grows out of the fact that we can perceive sequence between tones. Sequence means a perceived likeness in the degrees of difference between units. We saw in discussing rhythm that you have to have three repeats to establish the interval. Remember, too, that the sequence may be built out of repetitions of the same interval or out of proportionately increased or decreased intervals. What we really meant when we said that

93

PLATE IV

1. INTENSITY KEYS (from page 100)

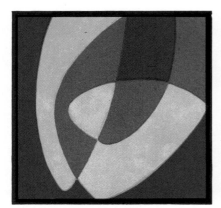

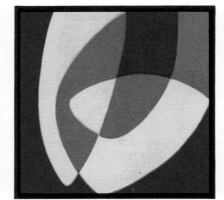

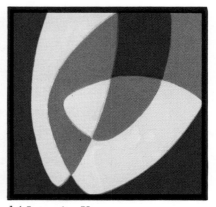

¾ Intensity Key   ½ Intensity Key   ¼ Intensity Key

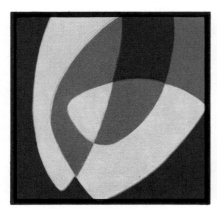

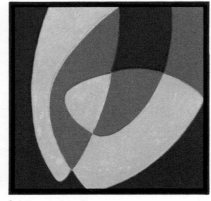

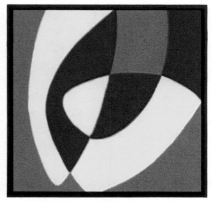

¼ Intensity Range   ½ Intensity Range   ¾ Intensity Range

2. COLOR HARMONY THROUGH DOMINANT LIKENESS (from page 103)

a   Monochromatic Scheme   b   With Variety Accent   c   Neutral with Variety Accent

PLATE V

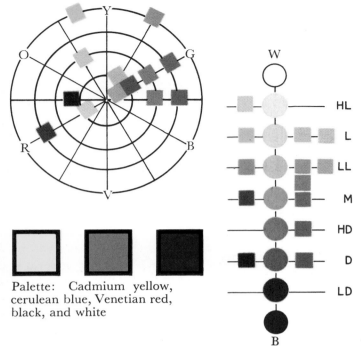

Palette: Cadmium yellow, cerulean blue, Venetian red, black, and white

1. LIMITED PALETTE (from page 104)
    Patterns on this and the following plates are by students at Newcomb College.

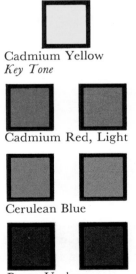

Cadmium Yellow
Key Tone

Cadmium Red, Light

Cerulean Blue

Burnt Umber
Unkeyed   *Keyed*

2. TONALITY TOWARD KEY HUE
        (from page 104)

95

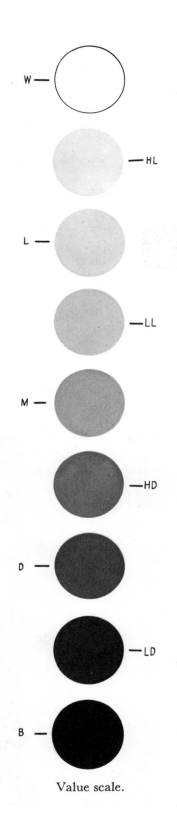

W —

—HL

L —

—LL

M —

—HD

D —

—LD

B —

Value scale.

there was an intrinsic order in the sequence of hues is that we recognize an equal and progressive degree of change from one to another.

Value

If we take three grays, A, B (a given interval darker), and C (darker than B by the same interval) the similarity of interval acts as a unifying factor in the pattern. We can establish these intervals at any given degree of contrast. Obviously, if they are small, there will be more similarity between the tones themselves. If they are great, there will be more variety between the tones, but the same tie-up in interval relationship.

It is convenient to have some sort of scale for giving these interval contrasts an objective value. To function, they have to be felt, but it is easier to talk about them if we can give them a name. Various color systems divide the total value range from white to black in different ways. It does not much matter how we do it so long as we understand the method. Such scales are essentially arbitrary but useful tools. We shall use the Ross-Pope* scale because it is simple and efficient. The diagram explains the division of the range into nine steps including white and black. The utility of such a scale is the basis for comparison that it offers. It seems to me sterile to use scales, as is often done in color theory, to write an abstract formula of value intervals which you then mechanically execute. I am sure it is much sounder practice to work out your intervals on the basis of direct perception and sensitivity. After all, this is the tradition. No first-rate painter or designer has ever depended on a mechanical system as a substitute for his sensibilities. The scale is helpful, though, as a checking device, and it gives us a precise language for discussing value relations.

Value Keys

We can go a step farther in organizing the problems of value interval. We shall use the value scale to make our discussion concrete. We do not have to apply these ideas by limiting them to the exact steps of the scale. Consider these patterns of relationship as typical of certain possibilities rather than as set formulas.

* Denman Ross, *The Theory of Pure Design*, Houghton Mifflin Company, Boston, 1907.
 Arthur Pope, *The Painter's Terms*, Harvard University Press, Cambridge, Mass., 1929.

HIGH KEY

If we restrict our value contrasts to roughly the upper third of the scale, say from white or high light down to low light, the result will be a pattern of high value key. (I am using the word *key*, a musical term, to indicate a characteristic relationship of tones; that is, a group of light values makes up a high key, and so on.) Within this range, we can set our intervals as we choose. We can use a regular sequence, a progression, or no definite interval pattern. There will be a unity from the necessarily close value intervals which we can reinforce by rhythmic interval relationships if we choose. Further, this high key has a definite expressive quality of lightness and delicacy that makes it suitable for certain purposes and unsuitable for others.

INTERMEDIATE KEY

If we restrict our contrasts to about the middle third of the value scale, another typical pattern emerges. This might range from, say, low light to high dark or dark. It again has a distinctive expressive quality, a certain restraint and refinement that can be very effective.

LOW KEY

If we work within the lower third of the scale, say from high dark to black, the result is a low value key. It has a muted and somewhat somber quality.

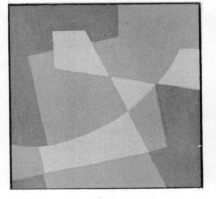

High key.   Intermédiate key.   Low key.

These ideas should not be used mechanically. It is perfectly possible to introduce small areas of greater contrast and still get the unity and expressive qualities of the typical patterns. It is also effective to combine the patterns in the same composition. This happens when you use two value themes, grouping one set of intervals in a high key, say, and another in an intermediate or low key. This is exemplified in Rembrandt's favorite method of handling

97

PLATE VI

1. TONALITY THROUGH DOMINANT
   TEMPERATURE (from page 105)

2. ISOLATION WITH BLACK
   (from page 106)

3. ISOLATION WITH WHITE
   (from page 106)

4. CONTRAST BALANCED WITH
   NEUTRAL (from page 106)

PLATE VII

1. ATMOSPHERIC PERSPEC-
TIVE and volume through spatial
effect of color (from page 118)

"View of Marseilles with L'Esta-
que" by Cézanne. (*Courtesy of the
Metropolitan Museum of Art.*)

2. MOTIF FROM A MOBILE LIGHT
COMPOSITION, Newcomb College
(from page 168)

3. SPACE THROUGH ADVANCING
AND RECEDING COLOR
(from page 118)

light. It is well, usually, to let one of the two themes dominate. Even that should not be taken as a definite rule. I have had students make beautiful organizations in which about equal emphasis was placed on both themes. It is a good guiding principle, however, to be disregarded only when you have a special reason.

The same idea can be applied to a wider total value range. You can break the scale into one-half or two-thirds divisions, keying these high, intermediate, or low. With the possibilities of increased contrast, your pattern will gain in strength, but sacrifice something of the subtlety and close-knit quality of the more restricted ranges. Or, finally, you can use the whole scale from white to black. Particularly in these latter cases, the use of definitely felt interval steps is important for unity.

One-half value range.

Three-quarters value range.

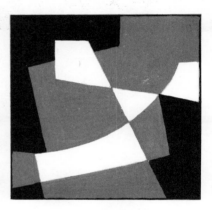

Full value range.

Intensity Keys

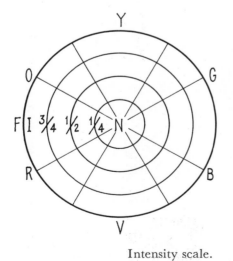

Intensity scale.

You can adapt the same methods to intensity relationships. The scale here is built on a series of concentric circles. Let the outside circle represent full intensities and the center point represent neutral gray. If we divide the radius of the circle into fourths and draw smaller circles through these points, we have a simple and practical scale. On it we can organize four intensity levels for each hue. (Each hue that comes at full intensity, that is. Many pigments give tones that will have to be placed within the outer circle even at their maximum intensity.) We can describe these levels in two ways: full intensity, ¾ intensity, ½ intensity, and ¼ intensity; or, working out from the center, ¾ neutralized, ½ neutralized, and ¼ neutralized. Some color systems, the Munsell for example, use more intervals. These scales are very valuable for the commercial standardization of colors. Our simpler one is quite adequate for our purposes and much easier to use.

100

The illustrations explain these possibilities more graphically than words could. I have applied the same organization we discussed for value to the intensity dimension. I want to underline three points. First, the expressive qualities of these typical patterns are quite distinctive. Second, what we said about freely interpreting the limitations of each scheme and about combining themes unified on different levels applies here, too. Third, the full intensity range does not, by itself, build unity. There is too strong a basis of hue contrast. We shall say more about the use of full intensities shortly.

*See Plate IV, 1
page 94.*

Hue Keys

This is the most complex of the three color dimensions to organize. Our difficulty is partly that *hue cannot be separated from value and intensity except analytically*. It is partly that the differences between hues are qualitative instead of quantitative. But we do perceive an intrinsic order in hue sequence. On the basis of this fact, we can apply the idea of interval relations.

Again we need a scale in order to be articulate about our problem. The hue circuit (that is, the spectrum tones plus the composite hues that lie between the ends of the spectrum) has been divided in many ways. Wilhelm Ostwald's scale is probably the most exact scientifically. He constructed it by measuring the threshold for perceiving the least possible difference between one hue and the next. It has twenty-four steps (by no means all the hues it is possible to distinguish) separated by equal intervals of contrast. While this scale is invaluable for color standards, it is rather complex and does not fit the tones of ordinary artists' pigments too well. The familiar twelve-hue division of primaries, secondaries, and tertiaries will serve our purpose.

ANALOGOUS INTERVALS

Whenever we build a hue pattern on small intervals, staying within less than a third of the hue circuit, we have a close-knit harmony. Analogous means like. The likeness between the hues in such an interval is strongly felt. For this very reason it is lacking in variety. You have to supply variety by contrast in other dimensions or by small notes of contrasting hue. One of the inaccuracies of our scale shows up clearly if we compare the analogous ranges from yellow to red-orange and from red to blue-violet with that from blue to yellow-green. Obviously the former are more analogous than the latter. The intervals in the Ostwald and the Munsell scales are more exact in this respect. The difficulty is not serious, however, since we are using the scale merely to indicate the possibilities rather than to plot actual patterns. When you understand

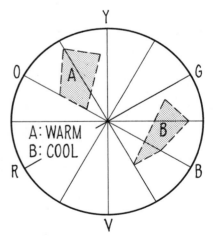

*See Plate II, 2
page 90.*

the principle, it is much more satisfactory to select a palette of pigments suitable for your purpose and let them set the range of intervals.

You can play with different rhythmic patterns in these intervals as we suggested for value and intensity. Since the intrinsic harmony between analogous hues is so strong, the harmonies of rhythmic interval are less essential than in the following keys.

TRIAD INTERVALS

Let us go a step farther with our idea of relationship through interval. We found that greater contrasts in value could be related by patterning the degree of change from one tone to another. The same thing holds for hue contrasts. If we use three tones separated by approximately one-third of the hue circuit, we make patterns based on the triad interval. The familiar primary and secondary triads are examples. These schemes have more variety. At the full intensity level, the contrast may well be stronger than the harmonizing quality. We have to be careful with our value and intensity contrasts not to make the variety too great.

This triad pattern, again, must not be interpreted too literally. We can use hues that approximate the interval. We can use a somewhat shorter interval between two of them with longer intervals to the third. The important idea is the principle of relating our tones by a felt similarity in the degree of difference between them.

This principle can easily be extended to patterns using more than three hues. We can relate four or five or more in the same way. We can do it by using approximately equal intervals or by using a progression of intervals.

COMPLEMENTARY INTERVALS

We said when we discussed the basis of this relationship that it was rather one of opposition than one of harmony. It gives us our greatest contrast in hue. We also found, in the last chapter, that complements have the effect of intensifying each other. Nevertheless, complementary intervals offer another important basis of harmony. When we control the contrast by means of relative amount and the other tonal dimensions, they can give a strength and vibrancy that nothing else affords.

Let me repeat the caution to base your use of complements on the true psychological complementaries. Not that you must always restrict yourself to them. When you are using off-complements and split-complements, though, you should know the true relationships. Then you can make the variations intentionally rather than by chance. (The illustrations show what we mean by off-and split-complements.) One more point: since the contrast between complements is so strong but at the same time so organically deter-

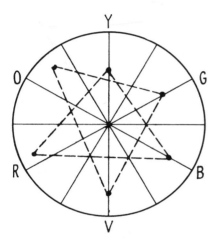

See Plate II, 2 page 90.

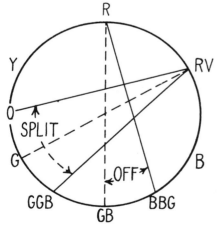

Off- and split-complements.

mined, the relationship has a special value. As a variety device, it helps us to give a clarity and luminosity to our color patterns that we cannot get in any other way.

COLOR TONALITY

We have considered separately these methods of relating our tones in each of the color dimensions. But in practice, we usually deal with them in relationship. We will not get far in studying the problems of tonality unless we realize the importance of the shapes, sizes, and positions of our color areas. This is another reason why theoretical harmonies are not very satisfactory. The quality of our organization will depend as much on how we distribute our tones as it will on the relationships between the tones themselves. In other words, composition is indivisible. The color relations, in practice, can not be abstracted from movement, proportion, rhythm, balance, and figure-ground. Obviously, though, these are too many balls to juggle at one time in a discussion. We shall have to be arbitrary. We shall concentrate on the tonal factors. It will be up to you to restore the unity between tone and form in your work.

Now, consider these problems of allover tonality. They divide naturally into two groups. In the majority of cases, our tonality depends on a dominant unity into which we introduce enough variety to serve our expressive purposes. In a smaller number of cases, we are working with schemes in which the expression depends on strong contrast and variety. Here our problem is to unify these contrasts. We have to keep them together in one composition without sacrificing their strength. We cannot begin to systematize every possibility in either of these categories. We shall be content to discuss some of the most important and characteristic possibilities.

Tonality Through a Dominant Unity

MONOCHROMATIC SCHEMES

One of the simplest ways of getting such a tonality is by the use of only one hue. This forces us to depend on value and intensity differences alone in building our pattern. The unity in hue automatically produces a harmonious tonality. We can, of course, do the same thing with neutral values.

See Plate IV 2 page 94.

This scheme can be varied by the introduction of subordinated contrasts outside the basic unity. We can add another color or a neutral to our dominant theme. In a neutral scheme we can introduce one or two subordinate hue notes. Such patterns do not have a great deal of variety, but they can be very effective.

103

LIMITED PALETTES

An excellent technical method for getting tonality is the use of a limited palette. When we analyzed the tonal ranges to be obtained from pigment mixtures, we saw how this works. Because of their semi-chrome character, pigments can produce only a limited range of mixed tone. This automatically imposes closer hue and intensity intervals upon the resulting tones. Just how close these intervals will be depends on the pigments you select for your palette. For example, the approximate triad we analyzed in Chapter 6 has a fairly wide range of hue, value, and intensity contrasts. If we substitute a more exact primary triad, say alizarine crimson, cadmium yellow medium, and ultramarine blue, the range will be much wider. But if we substitute a green-blue such as phthalocyanine blue in our first triad, the mixtures with cadmium red light and yellow ochre will give a much more restricted range.

See Plate V, 1 page 95.

It is significant that workers with color up to the nineteenth century always had the discipline of this method. Until the discovery of the coal-tar and other colors that have come out of modern chemistry, the number of pigments was small. You had to work with restricted palettes. More than that, many of the colors were available only in more or less neutralized form. You had to explore exhaustively the expressive resources within these restricted ranges. A feeling for the intrinsic relationships of different combinations was a natural result.

It seems to me that these facts offer a valuable lesson for us today. I know no better way of training one's color sensitivities than exploring such limited palettes. I would have you start with combinations of two hue pigments and black and white. Then experiment with three hues, and so on. When you have stored up a fund of such experience, you have a wealth of natural harmonies at your disposal. With such a basic control, you can then introduce more hues, either in mixture or by themselves, to get specific qualities you will want. You can control them because the limited basic palette establishes your fundamental tonality.

TONALITY TOWARD ONE HUE

A closely related possibility is the keying of your whole palette toward one of the hues. Technically you can do this in two ways. Take a specific example. Suppose we have a palette of cadmium yellow light, cerulean blue, cadmium red light, burnt umber, black, and white. You will see that this is approximately a major triad plus a neutralized, low-value orange in the burnt umber. There is plenty of contrast in it. We can proceed to key it toward any one of these hues by mixing a little of that hue into each of the other pigments. Suppose we key it toward yellow. The cadmium

See Plate V, 2 page 95.

104

red will be moved a little closer to orange. The cerulean blue will become a little greener. The burnt umber will turn into a slightly yellower brown. If white or gray is to be used by itself, it, too, can be keyed into the scheme. The effect will still be basically that of the major triad. But all the hue intervals will be shorter, and the yellow will serve as a common harmonizing factor.

The other method of keying the tones is to paint with the unmodified palette and then to glaze the whole pattern with a transparent wash of the key tone—another standard technique of the past.

TONALITY TOWARD A DOMINANT TEMPERATURE

Another rich possibility lies in the use of a dominant temperature. If you make the major area of the composition either warm or cool, the pattern will be tied together by a tonality of temperature. Into this you can then introduce complementary or neutral tones for variety. You can play with the idea of temperature themes, using a counterpoint between a warm theme and a cool one. It is safer to let one or the other dominate. It is possible, however, to have about equal emphasis between them, if you handle the space pattern well.

See Plate VI, 1
page 98.

Tonality in Patterns with Strong Variety

This problem is restricted to strong hue and intensity contrasts. Value contrast enters into it, of course. But where the contrast is primarily one of value, the ties in hue and intensity solve the problem. We all feel that some colors simply will not go together. If they meet edge to edge or one on the other, the hue and intensity contrasts are painful. Yet there are times when these acid combinations are exactly what we want. Our problem is to control the contrast enough so that it does not tear the composition apart, while retaining all the strength and vibrancy it can give. There are several ways in which we can do this.

SIZE OF AREAS

If the tonality of the pattern as a whole is established, we can use small accents of these over-strong contrasts most effectively. They function as absolute variety, and so do not, strictly speaking, come under our problem at all. This seems to be the best place to illustrate them, however.

See Plate II, 2
page 90.

ISOLATION OF CONTRAST

This is the basic principle. We can apply it in a number of ways. One very effective method is to use neutrals. If we reduce the area of contrast by separating part or all of the tones with a neutral line,

See Plate VI, 2 and 3 page 98.

we can get the contrast down to manageable limits. Black and white are the most effective neutrals for this purpose, because they are so positive in themselves. Gray can also be used, however. The great Gothic stained-glass windows are good examples of isolation with black. The saturation of the red, blue, and green light filtered through them would be unbearable if it were not for the isolation of the black leading. As it is, the jeweled brilliance of the color is miraculous. Such painters as Georges Rouault and Abraham Rattner exploit the same device for effects of richness obtainable in no other way. It should be noticed that the neutral has a structural and accenting function as well as serving to isolate the hue contrasts.

See Plate VI, 4 page 98.

Another method of applying the same principle is this: if we use the neutral as a background, dominating in actual area, unisolated contrasts can be placed in it. This is a favorite device of stage designers. A chorus line can be costumed in violently clashing colors—magenta and cerise, cerise and chartreuse, and so on, but if the background is dominantly neutral, the effect will be one of exuberance and exhilaration. You do not have to limit your neutrals to gray. Any hue that is sufficiently neutralized will also work.

What we have done in this chapter is to explore systematically some of the characteristic possibilities for getting unity into our color patterns. None of these ideas are rules. Their only value is as guiding principles to help you develop your own natural feeling for color relationships. I hope they will help you to become familiar with the complexities of the problem. They should increase your ability to be self-critical, and to know not only that something is wrong with your work, but also what is wrong and how to set about correcting it. They should enable you to get a lot more out of studying color patterns in nature and in the work of others. These two things will help you to handle color with distinction: (1) studying the relationships wherever color appeals to you and (2) practice and then more practice.

READING LIST

Graves, Maitland: *The Art of Color and Design*, McGraw-Hill Book Company, Inc., New York, 1941. Chapters 9 and 10.

Kepes, Gyorgy: *The Language of Vision*, P. Theobald, Chicago, 1944. Chapter 3.

Sargent, Walter: *The Enjoyment and Use of Color*, Charles Scribner's Sons, New York, 1923. Chapters 5 and 6.

PROBLEM VII

Purpose:

To explore some of the problems of tone relationship.

Problems:

1. Achromatic-chromatic composition. Make an abstract composition using a dominant achromatic theme. Include not more than three chromatic notes for variety and emphasis. Use a dominant key (high, intermediate, or low) for the pattern.
2. Monochromatic composition. Make an abstract composition using value and intensity variation within one hue. Include subordinate variety notes in a different hue or in achromatic tones. Key the composition in value, but use a different key from the first.
3. Make an abstract composition using a dominant warm or cool theme. Use tones from the opposite temperature group for variety. Use a full value range, but key your tones in a middle range of intensity contrast.
4. Complementary composition. Make an abstract composition using two sets of psychological complements. Let two of the related tones dominate. Feel free to use as many value and intensity variations of your tones as you need.
5. Limited palette composition. Select a palette of two hues and black and white. Work out your own pattern of dominance and variety. Try the same idea using three hues and four hues.
6. Tonality toward one hue. Select a palette of four or five hue pigments and black and white. Key your palette toward one of the hues by mixing some of it into your working stock of each of the other pigments. Work out your own pattern of dominance and variety.
7. Isolation of contrast with black. Select a group of full intensity tones for your composition. Deliberately include contrasts you consider unpleasant. By using black isolation between your areas, try to make a satisfactory color organization. You do not need to surround each area with black. Use isolation only where you want it. Do not overlook the structural and attraction values of black itself.
8. Isolation of contrast with white. Repeat the above problem using white instead of black for isolation.

   You might also try a composition using both black and white.
9. Accent with black and white. Make an abstract composition controlling your intensities so that isolation is not necessary. Use black and white for their accenting value. Study the differences in the quality of the black and white compared with 7 and 8.
10. Tonality with a neutral background. Make an abstract composition using a neutralized background. (This may be achromatic or a neutralized hue.) Use a wide range of strong hue and intensity contrasts in your figure elements. Your form will be equally as important as your color in these compositions. It is important to work out patterns that provide both variety in size of area and opportunity to repeat tones in different parts of the composition. Try letting some of your compositions grow as you paint. Start with a shape of some tone and build the pattern as you go.

Specifications:

1. Materials:
    a. Use a 10- by 15-inch sheet of illustration board for each composition.
    b. Paint with water color (transparent or opaque, or both in combination).
2. Presentation:
    a. Lay out a vertical format, 6- by 7½-inches, on the right-hand side of the board.
    b. Well laid out in the left-hand space, place the following: a 6-inch horizontal value scale; below it, a 4-inch circular hue and intensity scale. (See illustration.)
    c. As you work, make small swatches of each tone. Keep a sheet of scrap paper at hand for this purpose. After your composition is complete, cut two ¼-inch swatches of each tone from your scrap paper. Organize these on the two scales, one set to show the value relations of your tones, the other to show the hue and intensity relationships. These scales have two values. First, judging the qualities of your tones to fit them properly into the scales sharpens your sensitivity to color qualities. Second, your free feeling for color is not inhibited as you work, but you get the helpful discipline of systematically studying the relationships you have created after they are made. The charts will often be illuminating, both in revealing the basis of weaknesses in the pattern and in helping to show the foundation of its effectiveness.
    d. Include small swatches of the pigments used. Label them with their pigment names.

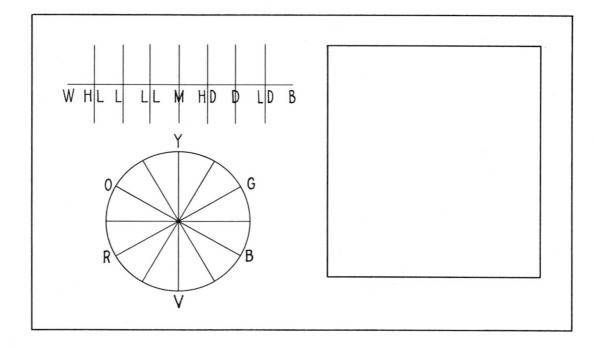

9 DEPTH

AND PLASTIC ILLUSION

Before we turn to the specific problems of three-dimensional organization, there is one more two-dimensional problem we should examine. As a matter of fact, it affords a good transition between the two. This is the means of creating an illusion of depth and plastic volume on a two-dimensional surface. We should not stress the word "illusion" too hard. As we shall see in a minute, "interpretation" might be a better word for what we mean.

Our actual experience of depth depends on two things: the direct awareness we have of three-dimensional space (clearly revealed in our perception of the homogeneous field), and the phenomena of disparity, accommodation, and convergence which we discussed in Chapter 3. None of these factors can act when we look at a two-dimensional pattern. Our interpretations of depth and plastic volume must be due to other factors.

BASIS OF SPACE ILLUSION

There are other characteristics of our visual field involving actual depth. The fact that the angle of light gathered by our eyes from distant objects is smaller than that from near objects; the fact of the overlapping of objects in the visual field; the fact of converging parallel lines; and so on. These are secondary indications of space.

Although these indications are present in the actual depth field and contribute to our perception, they are not responsible for our sensation of depth. This is shown clearly in stereopticon projection. If we look at the stereopticon slide itself, we interpret the depth in the pictures from these indications of space. That this is not a direct perception is evident when we look through the stereopticon projector. The prism lenses overlap the two slightly different views of the same scene in such a way that disparity is called into play. What before was at best an illusion of depth, we now see as actual three-dimensional depth. That this, too, is an illusion does not affect our point. Disparity acts here as it would if we were looking at the actual scene. This is really the only way we can create the "illusion" of depth on a two-dimensional surface. For the rest, we have to depend on an interpretation.

Perspective

From the time of the Renaissance, we in the West have depended principally on one method of organizing these indications of space into a coherent system of depth illusion, perspective. We shall not achieve creative freedom and mastery of space and plastic quality until we recognize that perspective is only one of a number of ways for making such an organization. We have to realize that our interpretation of space depends on the indications themselves, not on the particular method we use to organize them.

Our experience has been so conditioned by the conventions of one- and two-point perspective that it may be well to point out how arbitrary they actually are. We are accustomed to think that perspective renders things just as we see them. If you have worked very much with mechanical perspectives, you know how distorted they can be if you do not pick exactly the right station point and eye level for your subject. What we mean by saying that a drawing looks just like its subject is that it agrees with our visual concept, not that it reproduces our actual visual pattern. (To repeat, we see through our eyes but with our minds. Perception involves the whole pattern of nerve and brain response as well as the visual stimulus.) If we look fixedly at one point with one eye, our visual pattern can be reproduced by perspective. That is not the way we see things. We use two eyes and we continuously shift our focus of attention. Our impression of the scene is a mental concept. Perspective is as arbitrary a way of stating this mental concept as any other.

My purpose is not to disparage perspective, but to show that we cannot accept it as an end in itself, as the *only* basis for creating depth and plastic illusion. We can concede that as a method it probably comes closer to representing our visual impression of things than other methods. That only means that perspective is the best system when our purpose is literal accuracy. We must not confuse truth of appearance and expression. We can interpret depth by other methods of organizing the indications of space. The range of expression these other means give us is infinitely greater than that which we can get from perspective alone. We should understand them all so that we can make the best choice to serve our specific purpose.

INDICATIONS OF SPACE

We shall proceed with a study of the real basis of depth and plastic illusion, the indications of space. Five significant characteristics of the light pattern projected on our retinas are the physical bases of these indications of space. We shall discuss first the relevant characteristic of that light pattern, then develop the use of the space indications that grow out of it.

The first important fact about the projection of the visual field on our retinas is the disparity in the angles of light gathered by our eyes from near and distant objects. What the psychologists call the *constancy phenomenon* is a necessary part of our interpretation of depth from this disparity. If we look at two men, one 10 feet away, the other 20, the angle of light gathered from the nearer figure is twice as great as that from the farther. The projection of the nearer figure will occupy four times the area on the retina that the farther occupies. This difference is interpreted not as a big and a little man, but as a man of the same approximate size nearer to us and farther away. This is true because men have a constancy of size within relative limitations. The importance of constancy will be clear if we take the case of a large distant form such as a mountain. It may actually occupy a larger area on the retina than a house nearby. There will still be no confusion in reading the spatial order. This is partly because other indications such as overlapping are present, but chiefly because mountains belong to a different category of size from houses. An interesting use of the constancy phenomenon is this: architects usually include a figure in their renderings to "give scale." Painters and illustrators often use some familiar object—a human figure, a house, a tree, a vehicle, and so on—for the same purpose.

Now, let us see how this fact about our visual patterns can be exploited to create depth on a two-dimensional plane.

111

Contrast and Gradation in Size

If we establish a constancy between elements in our composition, either by representation or shape similarity, contrast and gradation in size will be interpreted as indications of space. The illustrations show how this works, both for representational subjects and for abstract ones.

Gradation. Advertisement for the Container Corporation of America, by Gene Walther. (*Courtesy of the Container Corporation of America.*)

Contrast. Advertisement for the Hawaii Tourist Bureau, by Melbourne Brindle. (*Courtesy of the artist.*)

Converging Parallels and Diagonal Movement

Perspective. "Prison," by Giambattista Piranesi, eighteenth century.

If we have a rectangular plane in actual space, receding into depth parallel to our visual axis, the angle of light gathered from the far end will be smaller than that gathered from the near end. This causes a distortion in the shape of the rectangle as it is projected on the retina. Unless they are very tall, the two vertical ends will remain vertical. Since they are seen as different lengths, the connecting top and bottom edges appear to converge as they recede. In other words, lines that are in fact horizontal and parallel appear to be converging diagonals. You can see that constancy is involved here too. Only if we read this pattern as a rectangle will it seem to recede.

In this example, two indications are combined—both contrast in size and converging parallels are involved. When we apply the principle to a plane surface, we can co-ordinate them as they are in our perceptions of actual space. Perspective does this. We can do the same thing arbitrarily without perspective. We can also abstract the dynamic movement of the diagonal line without convergence

112

and use it to create space. This is the basis of the familiar principle of isometric projection. It is the foundation for the handling of space in much Oriental art. The illustrations show how these possibilities work.

Arbitrary use of diagonals. "First Street Church, New Orleans," by the author, 1946.

Diagonal projection. "The Sleeping Elder Sister," by Haranobu. (*Courtesy of the Metropolitan Museum of Art.*)

113

Position in the Picture Plane

The horizon is always at our own eye level. The higher in the air we are, the more steeply the ground plane will seem to rise. As a result, objects at different distances away will appear to mount up higher with the ground plane. We can co-ordinate this fact with the other signs as we do in perspective. We can also use it by itself to create space. Historically, this has been a favorite device. You will find it in primitive, Oriental, Byzantine, medieval, and modern art. (Look at the advertisements in any magazine.) What we do is to tilt up the ground plane to occupy a good part of the picture plane. Then, by merely raising more distant objects higher than those close by, we create a sense of space and depth. We can co-ordinate this with contrast and gradation in size or not. Often, in the past, difference in size has been used with this scheme not as an indication of space but to show rank or importance. Note in passing that this device indicates depth without disturbing the flatness of the picture plane. We shall come back to this point later.

"Khusran and his Courtiers," by Nizami, about 1525. (*Courtesy of the Metropolitan Museum of Art.*)

"Dance of the Rooster," by Mario Carreño. (*Courtesy of the Perls Galleries.*)

114

The second important characteristic of the field with actual depth is *overlapping*. Objects at different distances from us are almost certain to overlap in their projection on our retinas. When one object covers part of another, we know from experience that it must be in front of it. Consequently, it is likely to be nearer. Let us see how this works in two-dimensional organizations.

We have already considered overlapping as a method of creating spatial tension in figure grouping. Depth, then, is not an inevitable interpretation of this device. We noted at the time, however, that it can be a powerful indication of space. If there is any tendency for the pattern to organize in depth (that is, if any of the other space indications are present), it is likely to function as a sign of depth, too. This is particularly true when it is correlated with contrast and gradation in size. The illustrations show how this works.

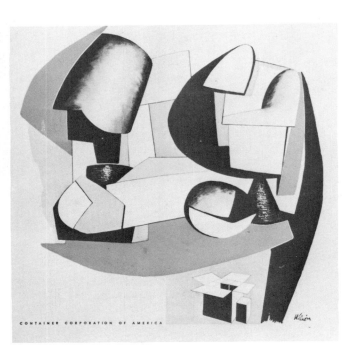

"Mountain Village," by Will Henry Stevens, 1939. (*Courtesy of the artist.*)

Advertisement for the Container Corporation of America, by Jean Hélion. (*Courtesy of the Container Corporation of America.*)

CONTAINER CORPORATION OF AMERICA

115

Transparency

Effect of transparency with construction paper. Class problem, Newcomb College.

An interesting variation of overlapping as an indication of space is the effect of *transparency*. We do not necessarily have to use actually transparent materials to get this effect. If the tone of an overlapping transparent area is adjusted between that of the top plane and that of the underneath plane, opaque materials will give the same effect. The most interesting characteristic of this device is the equivocal nature of the overlapping area. The tone, which has elements of the qualities of both spatial planes, is bivalent. It expresses two (or more) positions in space. This is the first example we have discussed of this bivalence in spatial indications. It is important as one of the characteristic developments in the contemporary handling of the space problem. Even though it is not a two-dimensional application, the way modern architects use transparency is interesting in this connection. The recent trend has been to use it in a new way. Glass ceases to be confined to windows. It becomes whole walls and partitions. The solid wall used to be accented with windows. Now the wall becomes an accent in a transparent plane. Spaces which are separated physically by these transparent planes are optically and psychologically united at a higher level of space organization.

The H. V. Manor House, Monte Vista, California. Clarence W. W. Mayhew, architect. (*Courtesy of the architect. Photograph by Roger Sturtevant.*)

116

In part, at least, the fascination and effectiveness of this modern feeling for transparency is an expression of the ratio of effort to accomplishment. The transparency gives to the same area two (or more) values in perception. It comes very near satisfying that eminently human desire to get something for nothing.

Diminishing Detail

The third characteristic of the visual field with actual depth is the correlation of visual acuity with distance. This means that the amount and definition of detail we can see depends on the distance of forms from our eyes. If they are close, we can see the detail clearly. As the forms move away from us, more and more of the detail is lost. At great distances, even the plastic form of a mountain disappears into mere outline.

The use of this indication in two-dimensional space patterns is simple and clear. The chief point I want to make is this: we probably have a tendency to think of this indication as applying chiefly to representational subjects. There is no reason why it should be so confined. We can use it with equal effect in abstract space patterns. We might apply it to visual texture, for instance. We could use a positive texture on a front area, a more subdued one at an intermediate depth, and an untextured or only slightly textured one in the distance. By itself, diminishing detail will not be read as an indication of space. We have to co-ordinate it with other indications. It is an effective additional resource, however. The illustrations show how it works.

"Abstraction," by Will Henry Stevens. (*Courtesy of the artist.*)

"Moonlight Scene at Nagakubo," by Hiroshige (1797–1858). (*Courtesy of the Metropolitan Museum of Art.*)

117

Atmospheric Perspective

The fourth significant characteristic of our visual pattern is the effect of light and atmosphere in our actual space field. The progressively deeper veil of atmosphere through which light has to travel from distant objects modifies their apparent tones and tone relations. All contrasts tend to diminish. The hue, value, and intensity relationships are pulled closer together. In the hue dimension, this is due to the cooling of all the tones. It is as if we looked at distant tones through a veil of sky color.

We can apply this phenomenon to the tone relations in two-dimensional patterns. Like diminishing detail, it does not create space by itself. When we co-ordinate it with other signs it is an effective additional resource. The impressionist painters made it the special focus of their handling of space. The basic principle was known long before the impressionists, however. A Sung landscape from China and the backgrounds of Florentine portraits will testify to this fact. Of all the signs we have studied, atmospheric perspective is most closely associated with representational effects. It need not be limited to them. We can use the same pattern of tone organization in abstract compositions just as effectively. The illustration demonstrates how it works.

See Plate VII, 1 page 99.

Advancing and Receding Tones as Indications of Space

The fifth characteristic of our visual pattern is of purely subjective origin. We discussed the basis of advancing and receding colors in Chapter 7. To focus red, we have to accommodate the lenses of our eyes in a manner similar to that for focusing near objects. For blue, the correlation is with distant objects. This fact, plus our associations with warm and cool tones, is the basis of advancing and receding color.

Temperature contrasts will not create space by themselves. They have to be organized to work with other space signs. Cézanne's exploration of these possibilities affords good illustration of this fact. It is true that he made a more detailed and conscious exploration of the effects of advancing and receding color than any other person up to his time. The impression one gets from much critical discussion of his work is that color alone creates the space and plastic volumes in his pictures. That this is not true is evident from a black-and-white reproduction. The form and spatial order are still perfectly clear, though often less positive. The abstract painters

118

have carried on this experimentation. You often find very interest- ing use of advancing and receding color to indicate space in their work. We should note that this possibility can be handled to suggest space without coming into conflict with the flatness of the picture plane.

See Plate VII, 3
page 99.

To sum up, we have eight distinct devices for indicating depth on a two-dimensional plane:
1. Contrast and gradation in size.
2. Converging parallels and diagonal action.
3. Position in the picture plane.
4. Overlapping.
5. Transparency.
6. Diminishing detail.
7. Atmospheric perspective.
8. Advancing and receding color.

CONCEPTS OF SPACE

We pointed out that perspective has dominated our Western space concept from the time of the Renaissance. Our analysis of space indications and the accompanying illustrations demonstrate the one-sided character of this domination. In freeing ourselves to make full, creative use of space, we have to get rid, not of perspec- tive, but of the preconception that it is the *only* method for organiz- ing depth. This is exactly what has been happening in the past few decades. Painters, illustrators, layout men, in fact, all who work with the two-dimensional surface, have been re-exploring the root causes of space illusion. Cubism gave a great impetus in this direction. Its influence has extended over ever broader fields. You cannot look through any contemporary magazine without realizing that perspec- tive is no longer an adequate basis for understanding what is done with the space problem. It is certainly no longer an adequate basis by itself for the creative handling of space.

In fact, one of the characteristics of our contemporary attitude toward the visual arts is the emergence of a new concept of space. This is what I have called a bivalent use of our space indications. We discussed it in considering transparency. The same idea can be extended to all the space indications. Many contemporary artists are exploring these possibilities. One thinks of Josef Albers, Her- bert Bayer, Moholy-Nagy, Gyorgy Kepes, Paul Rand, E. McKnight Kauffer, to name a few. We can call this new idea the concept of *equivocal space*.

119

Equivocal Space

We mean by this that the same signs give us two or more interpretations of space and depth. The familiar stair illusion is a simple illustration. We will interpret the bottom zigzag as being near or far, depending on how we organize the pattern in perception. If we do it so that we are looking down on the stair from above, the zigzag is near. If we do it so that we are looking up at the underside of the stair, the zigzag is away. The same line is bivalent, existing in a near plane and in a far plane. This is true of all the other lines in the pattern. The whole figure turns wrong side out when it changes. These optical illusions have been of great value to the psychologists in studying how our perceptions work. Now, we are discovering that we can use the same principle as an expressive resource in handling space. Alexander Dorner, in his book, *The Way Beyond Art*,* has made a very provocative and eloquent plea for this conception as the characteristic modern approach to space. While I do not care to follow Dorner all the way, it is true that equivocal space certainly opens up new creative potentials.

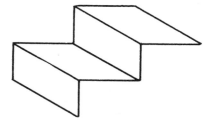

Step illusion.

"Steps," by Josef Albers, 1933
(*Courtesy of the artist.*)

Now we must examine a second major aspect of the whole problem.

* Alexander Dorner, *The Way Beyond Art*, Wittenborn, New York, 1947.

PLASTIC EFFECT ON A TWO-DIMENSIONAL PLANE

Space and volume are actually inseparable. We have continually had to make use of objects in our space to embody the indications we have discussed. These objects may be either two-dimensional planes or three-dimensional volumes. Let us see how we create these three-dimensional volumes and solids on a flat plane.

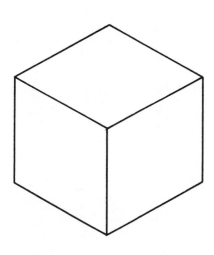

If we take a line drawing of a cube, for example, the pattern expresses a three-dimensional solid existing in space. It does so because the figure itself contains several indications of space: the activity of diagonals, gradation of measure, and overlapping. The last is there because we know the cube has a base and two sides hidden by the sides we see. Because of these space indications, the figure is more easily interpreted as solid and three-dimensional than as two-dimensional. We can see it as a flat pattern if we make sufficient effort of will, but, as the Gestalt psychologists would say, it makes a *better* pattern the other way.

Any plastic form on a two-dimensional surface depends basically on the presence of space indications in its make-up. We can carry the plastic quality further if we reinforce it by other means.

Structural Enhancement, Line

The first of these is the use of accentuation on the structural lines of the form. The line itself may be modulated in breadth and tone. The plastic quality of our cube can be increased by accenting the near lines, or by subtle modeling along the edges that express a change of plane. This device is particularly adaptable for line drawing. You will find it used throughout the course of civilization from the caves of Altamira to contemporary work.

Pen and wash drawing. "Woman Reading," by Rembrandt (1606–1669). (*Courtesy of the Metropolitan Museum of Art.*)

121

Structural Enhancement, Tone

A second step we can take is to separate the various planes with difference of tone. We do not need to model. If we do it properly, the simple contrast from one plane to the next will accent the structural lines. I said, if we do it properly. We have to be careful in using this device not to break up the unity of the form as a whole. If we keep the contrasts at the outline of the form greater than those within the form, we shall have no trouble. This method is particularly suited for poster and display designing, for which the flat color areas have good attention value.

"Ungheria," travel poster, by Uher. (*Courtesy of The Museum of Modern Art.*)

Chiaroscuro Modeling

A third means is *chiaroscuro modeling*. This means modeling in light and dark without regard to any definite light source. Gradation and contrast are organized to give a strong statement of structure. This emphasizes both the space indications and the ponderable, material qualities of the form. Since the organization of values is motivated solely by this objective, there need be no concern for logical light effect. We do not have to place all the light planes on one side and all the dark on the other. If we can make a stronger statement of the form by changing this order, there is no reason why we should not do so.

"The Echo of a Scream," by Alfaro Siqueiros, 1937. (*Courtesy of The Museum of Modern Art.*)

122

Finally, we can make use of the plastic effect of light to heighten the three-dimensionality of our forms. The light and dark is controlled by the light source (or sources) as well as by the form on which it falls. This sort of modeling can be abstract, in the sense that we can disregard cast shadow. This has the advantage of keeping the forms clear and simple, uncluttered by shadow patterns which are not significant. Where the cast shadows are helpful in describing the form, or where we want them for other purposes (design pattern, representation, or expressive values), they can be incorporated. (See the illustrations.)

Abstract lighting. "The Collector of Prints," by Edgar Degas. (*Courtesy of the Metropolitan Museum of Art.*)

Full effect of light with cast shadows. "Dancers Practicing at the Bar," by Edgar Degas. (*Courtesy of the Metropolitan Museum of Art.*)

DEPTH AND THE PICTURE PLANE

We are now in a position to consider this problem. It is only within relatively recent years that we have recognized that such a problem exists. Until the development of perspective, there was, generally speaking, no conflict between the means used to indicate depth and the flat nature of the picture plane. With that development, the plane tended to disappear. The format became a window opening into deep space. There was no picture plane in any but a physical sense. We are aware of a problem here because of our renewed search for the organic basis of depth illusion.

123

There are three characteristic attitudes we can take toward this problem. We can keep the plane flat, psychologically as well as physically. This means that we use only such signs of space as do not conflict with the nature of the plane. Historically, this has been the dominant attitude, to which Western art since the Renaissance is an exception. It is again a dominant trend in contemporary art. I do not mean in painting alone. It is as true of advertising art, display, layout, and so forth.

"Westwego in Red," by Will Henry Stevens, 1947. (*Courtesy of the artist.*)

Or we can deny the plane any psychological reality at all. We can make the format a window opening into deep space. In this case, we build our organization solely to exploit the depth illusion. For this purpose, the free use of perspective is our most effective system. Witness the tours de force of baroque mural decoration.

124

A painter such as Fra Andrea Pozzo could take the ceiling of St. Ignatius in Rome and dissolve it in a burst of glory. There is no ceiling left, just illusionistic architecture, clouds, light, and floating figures—a heavenly host glorifying St. Ignatius. Where you are concerned with deep space, there is no question but that you can treat the plane in this way. Until recent years, this has been the traditional approach in the West.

Finally, we can take up an intermediate position. We can keep some of the qualities of deep space but relate them to the picture plane in such a way that we do not deny its existence. We do this by emphasizing such indications of space as conflict least with the flatness of the plane, and by softening those that penetrate too energetically into space. Specifically, we can emphasize the planes in space that are parallel to the picture plane. We can soften diagonal progressions into space. The guiding principle is to conceive of

Ceiling of St. Ignatius Church, Rome, Decorated by Fra Andrea Pozzo, seventeenth century. (*Photograph by Alinari, Florence.*)

125

Photograph of Cézanne's subject at La Roche-Guyon. (*Courtesy of John Rewald.*)

"La Route Tournante à La Roche-Guyon," by Cézanne. (*Courtesy of Smith College Museum of Art.*) Comparison suggested by Erle Loran in *Cézanne's Composition.*

the space within the format as a definite volume, having a back, sides, and top. The movements into depth, then, will be resolved by returning them to the foreground. We do not let our space progress to infinity. If you compare the Cézanne landscape with the photograph of the subject, you can see clearly how he has handled his space with this limited concept in mind.

It seems to me fruitless to be dogmatic about the rightness or wrongness of any of these characteristic solutions of the depth–picture-plane problem. It is much more sensible to say that your purpose alone should determine the handling. Each method has its characteristic values and qualities. If you are illustrating a book page, there may be cogent reasons for maintaining the integrity of the surface in keeping with the type texture. If you are decorating a wall, there are surely strong reasons why the architectural solidity of the surface should be kept. On the other hand, we can cite distinguished examples of both these problems using the deep space approach. Everything depends, in the final analysis, upon the taste, sensitivity, and creative imagination of the designer. You are in a much better position to do what you have in mind, however, if you realize the conditions of your problem.

126

READING LIST

Berkman, Aaron: *Art and Space*, Social Sciences Publishers, New York, 1949.

Dorner, Alexander: *The Way Beyond Art*, Wittenborn, New York, 1947.

Kepes, Gyorgy: *The Language of Vision*, P. Theobald, Chicago, 1944. Chapter 2.

Koffka, Kurt: *The Principles of Gestalt Psychology*, Harcourt, Brace and Company, Inc., New York, 1935. Chapter 7.

Loran, Erle: *Cézanne's Composition*, University of California Press, Berkeley, Calif., 1944.

Rasmusen, Henry N.: *Art Structure*, McGraw-Hill Book Company, Inc., New York, 1950. Chapters 6–7.

PROBLEM VIII

Purpose:

To explore the problems of depth and plastic illusion on a two-dimensional surface.

Problems:

1. Make an abstract composition based on the theme "Things in Space." Conceive of your format as a volume of deep space, and put forms into it, using any of the indications of space you need to get your effect. Let some of your forms be flat, some three-dimensionally plastic. Use any means for achieving plastic illusion you may wish.
2. Make an abstract composition around the theme "Space in Things." Conceive of your format as an enclosed measure of space, like a box into which you are looking. Use planes and solids to give form and pattern to this space. In composition 1 you are concentrating on the spatial relationships of things. In this one you are concerned primarily with the three-dimensional form of space itself.
3. Make an abstract composition in which you use the effect of transparency to create the illusion of depth.

Specifications:

1. Materials:
    a. Compositions 1 and 2 should be done in pencil or charcoal on a sheet of suitable paper. The format should be no smaller than 12 by 15 inches.
    b. Composition 3 can be done on illustration board in poster color or can be made out of colored construction paper by cutting and pasting.
2. Presentation:
    a. Render neatly, allowing a sufficient margin to dress the composition.
    b. Title composition 1, "Things in Space." Title composition 2, "Space in Things." Title composition 3, "Space through Transparency."

10 THREE-DIMENSIONAL ORGANIZATION

The most vexing problem I have faced in writing this book is that of organization. The reason for this is the nature of designing itself. The problems of designing cannot be divided. There is no *one* logical beginning and no end ever. The structure that is essential for any coherent discussion has to be imposed. It is necessarily arbitrary.

I feel this very strongly in approaching the question of three-dimensional organization. Almost all the factors we have considered so far have to be treated again. There is no way around this dilemma. I had to choose between repetition and the complications of trying to discuss both two- and three-dimensional problems together. The former seemed the clearer approach. My decision was based on this fact: although balance, for example, is both a two- and a three-dimensional problem, the nature of three dimensions makes the attack quite different and much more complex. The same thing is true for all the other factors. Let us see what these differences are.

NATURE OF THE THREE-DIMENSIONAL PROBLEM

In working with two-dimensional patterns we need be concerned with only one relationship to the observer. The design has a single face, so to speak. This is an enormous help. All our problems can be solved in one frame of reference.

That is no longer true when we project our patterns into actual space. To compose our form, we have to consider it from all around. The same thing is true for an observer. He cannot understand or appreciate the form without looking at it from all sides. This means one very important thing, that we are dealing not with one static system of relationships, but with a series of systems of interlocking relationships. Of course, there is one fundamental system. Objectively it is the design. But this one composition has many different aspects, all of which much be composed in themselves. More than that, each view must lead us on into the next. Unlike the two-dimensional composition, which must stay within its format, the three-dimensional composition fails, however effective one view may be, if it does not lead us on to explore its shifting relationships. This is a challenging problem. The sensitivity and understanding we have been developing must be extended to this new system of relationships.

For this reason, a sculptor's stand is mounted on a swivel. He continually turns his composition as he works. He studies it from all angles. Every plane and contour has a new value and expression as he changes its relation to himself or his to it. For the same reason, architects use orthographic projection to separate the key views of their building and to study the relations between them. (We shall discuss the values of this kind of drawing in a minute.) They usually carry their study into a scale model, so that they can visualize these relations more accurately. Industrial designers use small plastic models in clay and complete mock-ups in plaster (or similar easily formed materials) for the same purpose. These plastic studies are very important. They help enormously in visualizing the complex relationships with which we are dealing.

ORTHOGRAPHIC DRAWING

You are probably familiar with the principles of orthographic drawing. If you are not, you should study them. This is not the place to go into the technical aspects of the problem. I do want to point out, though, what a help this kind of drawing is in visualizing three-dimensional relationships. The basic idea is to analyze the form into key views that can be drawn in two dimensions. The way these views are related on the paper shows how they organize in space. The basic view is usually the plan. You can think of this as the pattern the form makes on the ground. With this plan as a basis, elevations can be taken from any given direction.

129

Architects and industrial designers usually work with four key elevations corresponding to the four sides of a box. These views of the object can be amplified with sections through the form to show the relationships that are not otherwise clear. The ability to analyze your forms this way is essential in any kind of structural designing. Not only do you need such drawings to show how the thing is built, but they are invaluable as a technique for visualizing what you are trying to do.

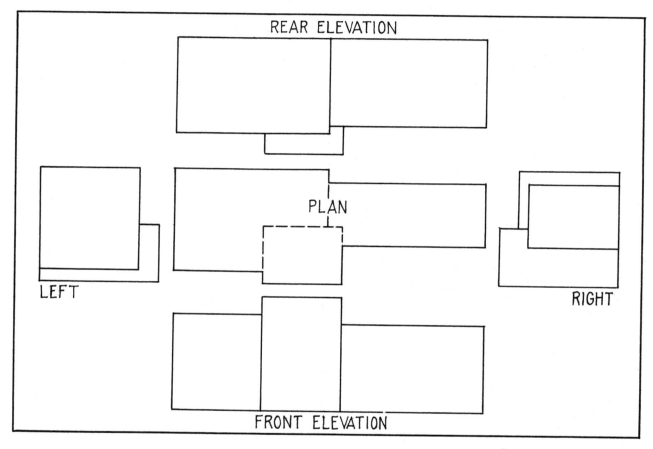

Orthographic projection.

THE PLASTIC ELEMENTS

First, I need to explain the sense in which we are using the word *plastic*. Literally, it means something you can mold, usually with your hands. Clay is plastic. Wax is plastic. The forms you make out of such materials have another characteristic. Being three-dimensional, they exist in space. When light falls on them, they are seen as a pattern of light and shade. It is in this latter sense

130

that we are speaking of *plastic elements*. We mean the basic elements out of which we can build a three-dimensional pattern. This pattern will be seen as a configuration of value contrasts and gradations when light falls on it. In this sense, any three-dimensional material that we can work, either by hand or with tools and machines, is plastic. These elements fall into three classes. By their action they give rise to a fourth nonmaterial plastic element. Let us examine them.

Solids

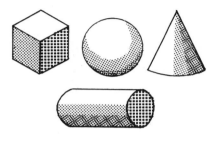

By a *solid* we mean something with bulk; something that expresses itself by projection in all the three dimensions of space. It may be solid all the way through like a block of stone. It may be hollow like terra cotta, or like a building. Its visual quality is the same.

Planes

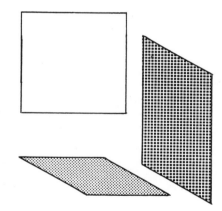

In geometry, a plane has only two dimensions, length and breadth. We cannot express a plane in space without thickness as well. It has to exist as material. The difference between a solid and a plane is relative. If the length and breadth dominate over the thickness, we perceive the form as a plane. We think of the Great Wall of China as a plane in spite of the bulk of material it contains. In other words, it depends to a great extent on the nature of the other elements in a composition whether a given form reads as a plane or a solid.

Lines

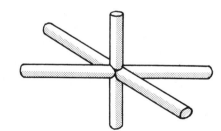

A line, in geometry, has one dimension only, extension. We cannot express this extension in material without giving it thickness. Again, the amount of mass such a form can have and still read as a line is a relative matter.

Space

The activities of our three material elements give rise to another. Space, itself, becomes a plastic element. In architecture, for instance, it is the *principal* element. The others are important chiefly as means for patterning space.

131

THE QUALITIES OF PLASTIC COMPOSITION

Before we tackle the specific problems of composing three-dimensionally, it will be helpful to consider the special qualities such patterns have. This will provide us with a general framework for our discussion.

Exterior and Interior Form

Most plastic compositions have two distinct formal aspects. We can think of them from the outside and from the inside. Some kinds of pattern have only one of these aspects. Sculpture, for example, generally deals with exterior form alone, although this is not necessarily true. In other cases, only the interior form is significant. One thinks of the rock-cut tombs of Egypt and of much theatrical and display designing. For the most part, both aspects are combined in the same composition. This is the case with architecture and industrial design particularly. Sometimes these two aspects are quite separate and distinct. At other times the two are closely related. This relationship, itself, may be a focal problem. The Gothic cathedrals illustrate the point. Their interior volumes—nave, aisles, triforium, transept, ambulatory chapels, and so on—are directly expressed in the exterior form. Contemporary architects employ transparency and penetration to achieve the same effect. (See the illustrations.)

Visual integration of interior and exterior form through transparency. The architect's home, Lincoln, Massachusetts. Walter Gropius, architect. (*Courtesy of the architect. Photograph by Robert Damora.*)

132

It will help us greatly in visualizing our plastic forms if we keep this distinction in mind. We shall see in a moment that the plastic elements have different activities in this respect. Much of their effect on space results from emphasizing their inherent interior form characteristics. We can almost say that space, as a plastic element, depends on these interior activities.

Closed and Open Form

The other general quality of plastic compositions has to do with the difference between closed and open form. Let us see what this means.

CLOSED FORM

Some kinds of plastic compositions appear to be controlled by a simple enclosing volume, usually geometric in nature. We can call this a *form envelope*. Everything happens inside it. Nothing projects beyond. This terminal surface of the form isolates it from surrounding space. Whatever spatial activity it may have is exerted within the envelope.

In architecture, we may take the Parthenon as an archetype. The rectangular solid of the cella surrounded by the colonnade and terminated by sloping roof planes expresses a simple form envelope. We feel the relationship of all the parts to this controlling concept. The typical New England Colonial house has the same quality. The trend in modern industrial designing is in the same direction. Take the automobile as an example. The assemblage of elements, the hood, passenger space, roof, fenders, and trunk were put together in the old models for function only. Visually they were an assemblage rather than a unity. What the modern designer tries to do is to tie all these elements together by making them express a single, unified form envelope. Sometimes we feel that he has become so preoccupied with this problem that he has forgotten some of the important functional requirements.

Whipple House, Ipswich, Massachusetts, about 1650.

1912 Oldsmobile.

1950 Studebaker. (*Courtesy of the Chivé Motor Company, New Orleans, Louisiana.*)

133

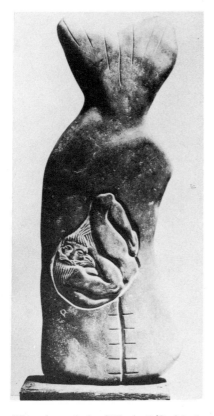

"Jonah and the Whale,"(Rebirth Motif), by John Flannagan. (*Courtesy of Mr. and Mrs. Milton Lowenthal. Photograph by Soichi Sunami.*)

Pre-Columbian Jaguar, Costa Rica. (*Courtesy of the Museum of Natural History, New York.*)

In sculpture we meet the same approach. Particularly when carving directly in stone or wood, sculptors often try to keep the sense of the block as a terminating envelope. John Flannagan's work is interesting in this respect. He used to collect field stones whose natural, weather-worn shapes suggested a subject to him. He would bring this concept out of the stone with as little carving as possible, leaving as nearly as he could its original natural volume. "Jonah" is a good example. I do not mean to imply that you have to take your form envelope ready-made. The pre-Columbian "Jaguar" might have been carved from an egg-shaped stone or from a square block. There is no escaping the power of the ellipsoidal envelope that controls the finished form.

If we think over the examples discussed, we see clearly that when we control our plastic composition with this sort of envelope, there is a characteristic resulting expression. Our form has a close-knit quality. It is *closed* away from surrounding space. It is dense and compact. This suggests that some subjects are adaptable to this treatment, others are not.

OPEN FORM

Open form is the antithesis of the preceding. The controlling factor here is not an enveloping volume, but a central core that may or may not be expressed. The thrust and movement of the elements work toward or away from it. The characteristic pattern has much more in common with the growth forms of nature. Such forms are not isolated from surrounding space. They reach out into it. It is often hard to say just where their activity stops. The separation between the exterior and interior aspects of the form is less marked. Both are likely to be so closely related that it is arbitrary to say this is exterior or that is interior. We shall illustrate again from architecture and sculpture.

Open form is the characteristic trend in contemporary architecture. This is true both in planning and in the visual composition. I think our new feeling for space has a lot to do with this. We are no longer content to live in a series of isolated boxes with openings for little peeps out. We have developed the means for heating and cooling unlimited volumes of space. We are no longer forced to huddle around the fireplace or stove for comfort. Our new resources for an environment of complex, interlocking spaces; spaces that flow into and out of each other; spaces that can be separated or joined at will; spaces that unite the inside with the outside, that bring nature in and living out—all of these are exciting to us. There are times when we still feel like crawling into a hole and pulling the hole in after us. We can provide for this in our new

134

architecture. The point is, we do not want to live that way all the
time. We also enjoy the freedom that open form makes possible.
Contrast the New England Colonial house with Frank Lloyd
Wright's Kaufmann house. In the former, the simple rectangular
envelope imposes a rigid limit on the planning of the space. You
have to have a series of regular cells with strong enclosure. The
latter is free and flexible. The planes and masses grow out from
the central core in response to an informal organization of space.
The house grows out of the landscape. It seems as much a part of
the environment as the waterfall on which it is poised.

The Kaufmann House, Bear Run, Pennsyl-
vania. Frank Lloyd Wright, architect,
1937. (*Courtesy of the architect.*)

135

Lipchitz's "The Rescue" shows the same kind of open approach. The masses are open. They are honeycombed with penetrating space. They reach out like the pseudopods of an amoeba to encompass surrounding space. It is impossible to define any enclosing envelope. The forms are controlled by the dynamic movement out from a perceptual central core and back to it again.

Our discussion has pointed up the expressive values of this sort of composition. It has also emphasized the strong spatial activity inevitably involved. Keep these four concepts in mind: exterior form, interior form, closed form, and open form. They will help to make our next points much clearer.

"The Rescue," by Jacques Lipchitz, 1945. (*Courtesy of the Bucholtz Gallery, New York. Photograph by Adolph Studly.*)

VISUAL STRUCTURE OF PLASTIC ORGANIZATION

We approached the whole problem of visual organization from the angle of the figure-ground pattern of our perceptions. Our next step was to explore the principles of figure organization. We shall use the same method in approaching three-dimensional organization.

Figure-Ground Organization

Carved plaster relief by a Newcomb College student.

Consider a bas-relief. We can think of it as a transitional form between two- and three-dimensional patterns. The figure elements have become plastic to some extent. They have depth. They are modeled by light. But they are still connected to a physical ground. Much of the detail in architecture and interior design has the same character. The chief difference from straight two-dimensional pattern is the use of plastic light and shade to define the figure. Such compositions still have but one face. They do not involve that system of multiple relationships which we found was the specific characteristic of three-dimensional compositions.

When we free our figure elements from a physical ground, a new condition arises. As far as our visual pattern is concerned, we still perceive the form because of figure-ground organization. The con-

136

trast between material and space defines the form. But now the ground can no longer be thought of as a physical part of the pattern. It is precisely this fact—that the ground becomes a purely psychological factor—that makes the problem so complex. These facts would have little significance for designing except for one circumstance.

Space Closure

When we were considering figure-ground before, we found a particular significance in the phenomenon of closure. To review briefly, if we draw a closed line figure, an interesting thing happens. The paper inside the line is seen as figure. The line reads as its boundary. The enclosed area seems to lie on top of the surrounding paper. This is complete closure. But we found that closure does not have to be complete to give this effect. Whenever we define an area of ground (give it a good shape and definite size), it will be incorporated as a figure element. The same principle operates with three-dimensional designing. This puts the plastic figure-ground problem in a new light. It is the basis on which space itself becomes a plastic element. Complete closure as a way of defining space is obvious. What is less obvious is that partial closure can also be used to define space. It is now time to study this problem. We shall take up each plastic element in turn.

SOLIDS

By its nature, a solid is likely to be a closed form. If it is made up of plane surfaces, it efficiently encloses space. But it does not, by itself, do much to define the space around it. Whatever defining power solids have usually comes from the way they are organized together. The patio in a U-shaped house is an example of a space volume defined by solids. The voids in a colonnade are similarly defined. In both examples it is not the individual solids but the relationship between them that does the defining.

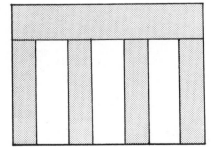

PLANES

A plane cannot by itself enclose space. It is true that a curved plane returning on itself does do this. The expression of such a form, from the outside at least, would be that of a solid. The potential of planes for *defining* space, however, is much greater. To understand this we need to examine some of their spatial characteristics.

137

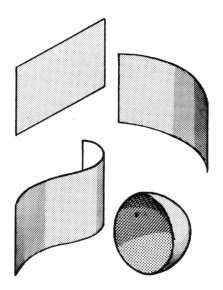

1. SHAPE. I am using the term *shape* in a special sense here. The difference between a rectangular plane and a circular or free-form shape makes little if any difference in its potential spatial activity. By contrast, whether the plane is flat or curved is most significant. It is the shape of the plane as it relates to all three spatial dimensions or to two only that determines its activity.

A flat plane in itself is neutral in spatial activity. It has neither an exterior nor an interior aspect. It is just a plane. When it is curved, though, the story is different. Now the plane has a definite exterior expression on the convex side. The concave side has a strong interior expression. It defines a space volume of positive shape and size. If we use an S-curved plane, the two expressions are combined. Both sides have elements of exterior and interior spatial activity. In a plane curved in two directions at the same time—a hemisphere, for instance—the exterior and interior form aspects are very positive. The space is strongly defined on the concave side, almost enclosed.

2. POSITION. The position of the plane in the space field is important in its power to define space. We need not consider its relation to the observer since this is a variable. For the same reason, we do not need to consider the depth dimension of space. In three-dimensional patterns, there is a continual change of value between width and depth. When we face the surface of a plane, its width is directly expressed. When we face the edge of the plane, it is expressed as depth. The same thing is true, of course, for solids. What is width and what is depth depends on how we look at the form. This leaves three key relations to the space field for us to think about—horizontal, vertical, and diagonal.

Since any three-dimensional composition has to exist in relation to gravity, the base of support necessarily enters into our consideration. This may be the ground, the floor, a pedestal. It is always there. It may not be expressed directly, as when the construction is suspended. The gravity relation will still be present and will act more or less positively. Let us examine the cases in which it enters directly into the pattern.

Suppose the plane in question lies on the horizontal base. Although, in a sense, the pattern is two-dimensional, it does define three-dimensional space. Let our plane be a tennis court, and you will see what I mean. The definition is not very strong, because only two of the dimensions are given. Nevertheless, the space over the court is different from that outside. It is playing space. It is "in bounds."

Now raise the plane above the ground. The space volume between is strongly defined. The length and breadth of the plane give us two dimensions of the space. The height from the ground gives us the third.

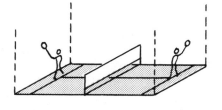

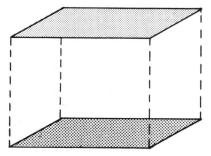

138

When we rest a vertical plane on the base, the definition is less complete. The plane and the ground define two sides of a volume, but the remaining sides are indefinite. If we raise the vertical plane in the air, the definition is weaker still.

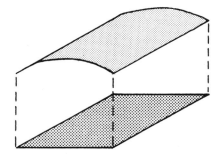

Diagonal planes vary between these two extremes. The more nearly they approach a horizontal position above the base, the stronger their spatial activity is. The more nearly they approach the vertical, the weaker it is.

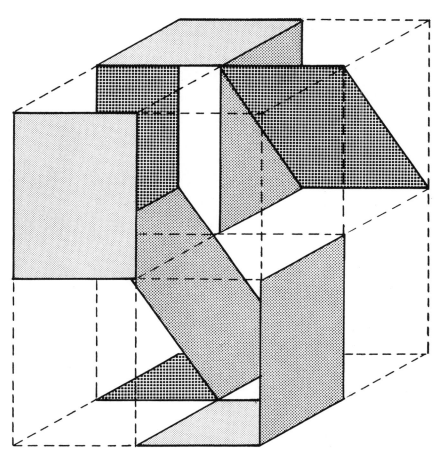

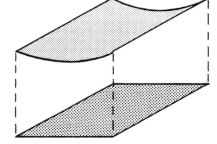

The shape of the plane modifies these basic patterns. Our discussion was based on a flat plane. If we substitute a curved plane, it makes a great deal of difference where the concave and convex sides are placed. Take one example to illustrate. Suppose the plane is parallel to and above the base. If the convex side is down, the spatial definition is weaker than that of a flat plane, because the volume of space is a less "good" shape. If the concave side is down, the definition is stronger. The space defined by the plane alone is united to that defined by the plane and the ground.

139

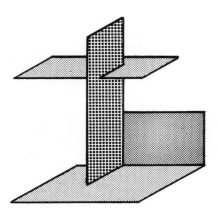

3. RELATIONSHIP. Position is one sort of relationship; it involves the base. When two or more planes are related to the base and to each other, the possibilities of spatial activity are greatly extended. Two vertical planes or a vertical and a horizontal plane obviously give us more resources to work with. The principle should be quite evident. The planes define a volume of space by giving us definite values for its three dimensions and by indicating its shape from their own sizes and relationships. Wherever such volumes of space are defined, the form will take on an interior expression.

LINES

First a word about the nature of lines as plastic elements. We have to distinguish between two kinds of linear elements. First, the edges of solids, the edges of planes, and the joinings of these elements make lines. Such lines are important as compositional elements. They contribute greatly to the expressive qualities of the form as well. They do not, by themselves, have much spatial activity. It is the other kind of plastic line, the line that exists by itself in space, that is significant here. It may be a girder or a cable or a rod. Whatever its material nature, if the linear extension predominates over width and depth, the form will read as a plastic line in space.

Visually, the primary expression of such lines is one of defining space. They are too thin to have much plastic quality in their own right. Like a line on paper, however, they effectively bound areas and volumes.

We rarely use such linear elements by themselves. They usually function with solids and planes as structural elements in the pattern. We shall take up this structural question later. For the moment, our interest lies in the fact that such plastic lines have great spatial activity.

VIRTUAL PLANES

This is not true of an isolated line in space any more than of an isolated line drawn on paper. The potential space-defining power of a line is realized only when it works in organization with other lines or planes. This leads us to the very interesting problem of *virtual planes*, that is, planes that have visual but not physical reality. If we anchor two vertical pipes in the ground and join their tops with another pipe, the plane of space they bound is a virtual plane. It has no physical reality. But, perceptually, it takes on much the same quality as the shape enclosed within a line on paper, though its special identity is not as strong. If we use several verticals, spaced at intervals, the virtual plane becomes very positive indeed. The same thing would be true if we substituted several horizontal elements. I choose the verticals because I want to make the point that such a plane need offer no hindrance to our movement in space in order to function visually. A fence or a lattice is an excellent example of a plane defined by plastic lines. But either is also a real plane, in that we can not walk through it. It is perforated rather than solid. A colonnade, however, is a true virtual plane. It exists only visually.

Plastic lines can be organized into both types of plane. They can form planes of any shape, position, and size. They can be flat, curved, or twisted. All we have said about actual planes applies equally to them. Added to this is the fact that they are always more or less open, therefore transparent. Because of this, we can use them in an equivocal manner. We can separate spatial volumes and join them at the same time. Like transparent planes of glass, they are one of our favorite tools in modern space composition.

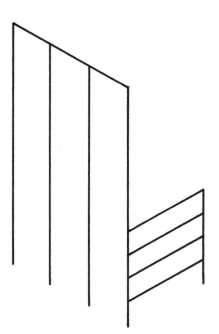

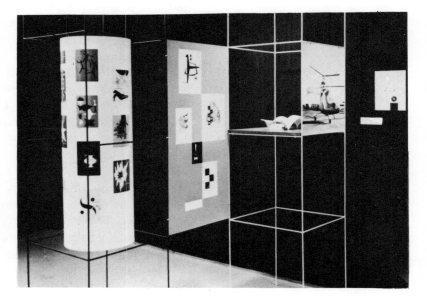

Mounting for traveling exhibition. Designed by Alvin Lustig. (*Courtesy of the designer. Photograph by Ben Rose.*)

PLASTIC FIGURE ORGANIZATION

The same two factors that we discussed before apply in three dimensions—likeness and spatial grouping. Having covered this ground from the angle of our visual image, all we need do now is to see how the plastic nature of our figure elements affects these two bases for grouping.

141

Likeness in Plastic Elements

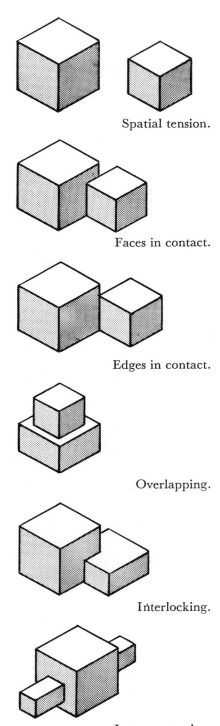

Spatial tension.

Faces in contact.

Edges in contact.

Overlapping.

Interlocking.

Interpenetration.

Let us quickly review our previous findings. We saw how we can tie our figure elements together by any recognizable sameness in their qualities. We classified these qualities under the headings of form, tone, and visual texture. I think the best way of applying these ideas to plastic form is to discuss a specific example. In the illustration I have analyzed a terra-cotta group by Jules Struppeck. Each diagram abstracts a different similarity element. We see how the possibilities are enriched over two-dimensional compositions. The fact that we must consider these relationships from many angles instead of one gives each part of the form many values.

Spatial Grouping of Plastic Elements

Grouping is extremely important in plastic composition for two reasons. First, there is no format to define the visual field. Our figure groupings have to be close-knit enough to stand the competition of other objects in the field. Second, the feeling for actual stress and weight in our materials is much stronger than in comparable two-dimensional forms. Our visual judgments of unity are strongly influenced by this fact. The parts must look as if they would stay together as well as be physically able to do so. An illuminating story in this connection is that of the first responses to Robert Maillart's bridges. They looked so ethereal and lacelike that people accustomed to heavy masonry and concrete forms were afraid to use them. Of course, I imply no criticism of Maillart's design. When the strangeness of the new forms wore off, we began responding with excitement to the relationships revealed. His work stands as a monument to creative imagination and understanding of materials. The point is that plastic unity in three dimensions has to be more close-knit in the tying of elements together than in two-dimensional patterns. We cannot depend on the isolation of the format or frame. We are working with actual weight and stress.

The basic possibilities for spatial grouping are the same as with two-dimensional elements, except that one new one is added. We can relate the elements by face-to-face contact. The diagrams analyze the basic possibilities.

In the next chapter, we shall take up the questions of unity and variety in plastic composition.

142

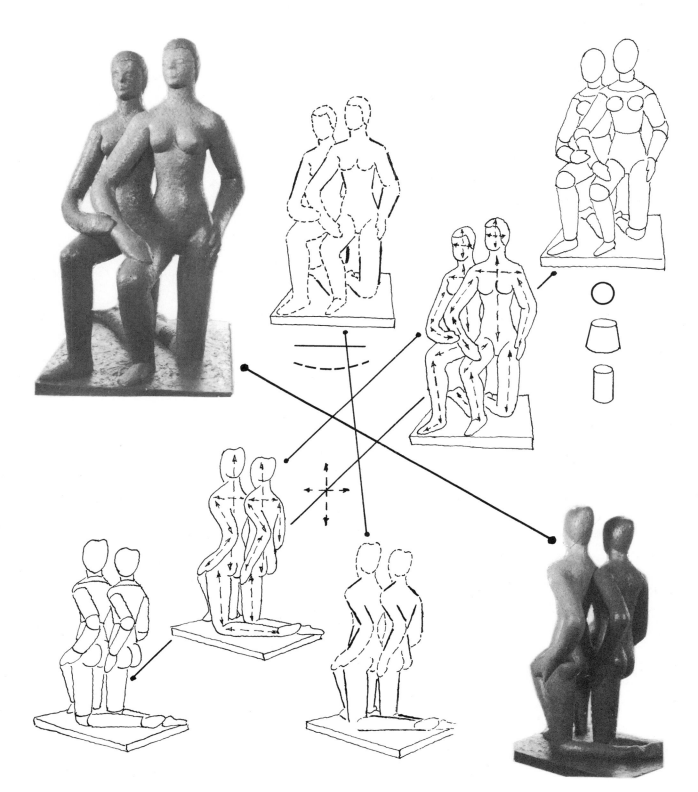

Terra-cotta group, by Jules Struppeck, 1948. (*Courtesy of the artist.*)

143

READING LIST

Giedion, Siegfried: *Space, Time, and Architecture*, Harvard University Press, Cambridge, Mass., 1941. Part VI.

Moholy-Nagy, L: *Vision in Motion*, P. Theobald, Chicago, 1947. Section on Sculpture.

Van Doren, Harold: *Industrial Design*, McGraw-Hill Book Company, Inc., New York, 1940. Chapter 9.

PROBLEM IX

Purpose:

To explore the problems of plastic relationships between solids and between planes in space.

Problems:

1. Plastic solids in space. Design and construct an abstract plastic composition composed of three simple geometric solids. One of the solids can have a hole in or through it. This gives you the resource of a void to use for accent.

Specifications:

1. Materials:
   a. Make your solids out of a sturdy cardboard (illustration board is fine for rectilinear forms) or out of balsa wood sheets.
   b. You can join the planes neatly with airplane cement, or fasten them with gummed paper tape. If you use the latter method, you will have to paint the composition to cover the tape.
2. Presentation:
   a. Great care should be taken in laying out your forms with precision. Consider the thickness of the materials in making your measurements.
   b. Plan the assembly carefully. It is a good procedure to tape as many of the joints as possible from the inside before your form is closed up. Cement the remaining joints neatly. If the parts have been cut with precision, you should have little trouble.
   c. The scale should be such that your form will fit within approximately a cubic foot of space. In other words, make it neither too large nor too small.
   d. Consider carefully the structural character of your design. Be sure that your form is imagined in the materials you use. For example, if you tried to contact the corner of one cube to the face of another, you would be in trouble. The point-plane contact is not structurally practical. You should modify your idea to use penetration. Let enough of the corner penetrate the plane for a good structural joint.
   e. *Keep it simple.* There is enough variety in the fact of its three-dimensional nature. Only when the composition is simple can you really study the proportion, rhythm, movement, and balance problems properly.

2. Plastic planes in space. Design and construct an abstract plastic composition composed of four rectangular planes, one vertical, one horizontal, and one depth plane. These are to be designed in relation to a rectangular base plane. One plane may have a hole in it. This gives you the resource of a void for accent. The shape of the hole may repeat the rectangular shapes, or contrast with them.

Specifications:
   1. Materials:
      a. Use planes of stiff cardboard or sheets of balsa wood.
      b. Join with airplane cement.
   2. Presentation:
      a. What was said above about technique applies here as well.
      b. Scale should be in keeping with the material. Depending on the emphasis in the design, the longest dimension should probably be less than a foot.
3. Plastic solids and planes in space. Design and construct an abstract plastic composition composed of solids and planes. There are no specific limitations on the number of elements, *but keep it simple.*

Specifications:

The points made above apply here. Do the most finished work in construction of which you are capable.

11 THREE-DIMENSIONAL ORGANIZATION (Continued)

Our means of creating unity in material forms in actual space are the same as in two-dimensional designing—movement circuits, balance, proportion, and rhythm. But the multiple values of our elements make these patterns of relationship richer. They also make them more difficult to handle.

Before we study these problems in detail, I want to expand a point we made at the end of the last chapter. We saw how the physical weight and the stresses in our materials affect figure organization. They have an equal effect on our other means of creating unity. This is not actually a new problem. We discussed its two-dimensional counterpart when we were studying attraction and attention value. (Remember the pyramid balanced on its point.) However, in two dimensions these qualities of weight and stress are associations, while in three dimensions, they are actual.

This fact has a bearing on more than the problem of structural relationships. When we were talking about organic unity, I used the jellyfish illustration to make the point that natural forms are material diagrams of force. They express the balance between the interior forces of growth and the exterior forces met with in the environment. We saw how the visual unity of such forms develops out of that balance. There is a parallel here with the balance between structural and visual relationships in plastic design. Support

146

must be physically equal to the load it bears. It must also look equal to the load it bears. On the other hand, it must not be disproportionate to its load. Nothing is more ridiculous than a monumental support with no load or with a delicate load. Our sense of fitness is outraged.

The same points are true of the other stresses. A tension member or a joint under torsion or shear must be physically sound. It must also look sound. Our habit of feeling ourselves into the structure, of responding empathetically to the work members do, makes it impossible to consider problems of balance or movement or proportion without taking these factors into account.

One final point in this connection: we respond sensitively to the proportion of effort to accomplishment. Throughout history, there has been a search for the most economical balance possible. You can see this in the development of Romanesque architectural forms into Gothic forms. The contrast we drew between the Louis XIV and Louis XV chairs illustrates the same search. Maillart's bridges are expressions of a like development in the use of ferroconcrete. Our modern architecture reflects this value of economy of means. The characteristic attitude toward space is only one example. As always with a new idea, modern architects developed an economy in the structural use of steel construction before they dared give it visual expression. Our earlier skyscrapers were structurally exciting, but this value was buried at first under a veil of stylistic clichés. It takes time for us, designer as well as consumer, to appreciate the visual values of a new balance between effort and work done. The creative and imaginative designer makes the first response. He dares to reveal these new forms. Gradually the rest of us follow along. Our empathetic responses are educated to this more perfect balance of effort and accomplishment. The beauty of the new form moves us.

We conclude, therefore, that the problems of plastic unity are inseparable from structural problems of weight and stress. At the same time, we cannot say dogmatically that any one formal solution of these problems is ultimately right. Actually we are only repeating in new words one of the premises from which we started, that a form to serve our purpose cannot be conceived independently of materials and techniques. Real creative imagination means visualizing through material and technical processes. We have to think plywood thoughts or ferroconcrete thoughts. When we do that, the bond between structural and visual relationships is direct and organic. It is necessary to reaffirm this because we can so easily think of our formal principles of unity as self-sufficient. We are always in danger of trying to apply them to a structural system instead of bringing them out through the structure.

Cathedral of Angoulême, twelfth century. (*Photograph by Giraudon, Paris.*)

Amiens Cathedral, thirteenth century. (*Photograph by Clarence Ward.*)

147

PLASTIC MOVEMENT CIRCUITS

Linear Elements

The most obvious plastic resource for building closed movement circuits is line. We have distinguished two sorts of linear elements, those that are expressed by the edges and meetings of planes, and those that are expressed directly in material. To these we can add decorative lines. These can be plastic (moldings, flutings, string courses, and so forth) or they can be created by tonal or textural contrast. In a sense, these latter lines are two-dimensional, even when they have plastic projection. Their primary function is to decorate the surfaces of the plastic form. Nevertheless, they are part of the whole composition. They can be woven into the major movement patterns and rhythms. We can say dogmatically that only when they are treated in this way or have a structural reason behind them, do they have any place in the composition. One of the besetting sins of contemporary industrial design is the plastering on of meaningless decorative lines such as streamlined fluting on food mixers or excessive chromium streamlines on cars.

I slipped in another qualification in the last paragraph. Decorative-structural line sounds like a paradox, but there are times when we do have that combination. A sheet of corrugated or fluted metal, for example, is strengthened enormously in one direction. Such decorative linear treatment of the surface also serves a structural function, or vice versa.

Axial Elements

Solids and planes express movement in their linear outlines. They also express it in their dominant axes. A tall vertical mass has an ascending movement. The same form in a horizontal position has a lengthwise movement. Curved surfaces, either in solids or planes, express a double movement, in that they turn toward or away from us.

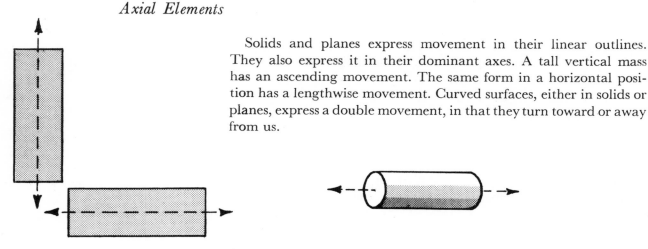

148

Movement is always involved in sequences of progression and alternation. We can express these in the plastic elements themselves or in the accents with which we treat the elements—windows and doors in architecture, for example.

Patterns of Attraction

What we said in Chapter 4 about using the attractions of tonal and textural contrast to reinforce our linear and compositional movements applies here as well. We should note that visual texture is relatively more important here. We have a greater range of materials to work with in three dimensions than in two. Since our materials are three-dimensional, we also have a greater control over textures applied to their surfaces. One thinks of the texturing of plaster or stucco or the rustication of stone. It is true that these practices tend to be less used. We are much more interested in the intrinsic textures—wood grain, plastics, and other synthetics, for example.

The problem of composing these movements into a patterned circuit is essentially the same as it was in two dimensions. What we said there applies here as well. The difference, as always, is that we have to consider the movement from many angles in relation to the third dimension.

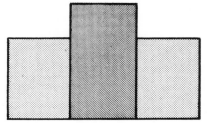

PLASTIC BALANCE

Our classification of the types of balance into axial, central, and occult will serve us again. It is very important to realize, however, that different types may be involved in the same composition. Since our composition breaks down into a series of views, a symmetrical organization in one view may no longer be symmetrical in another. The human body is a clear example of this fact. From the front and back we are symmetrical. From the sides, our body masses are asymmetrically related. We can see the same thing in architectural compositions. Formal buildings are often symmetrical in front view. From the side and back they may or may not be so. The illustration shows this change in the principle of balance as we move around a building.

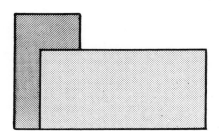

Axial Balance

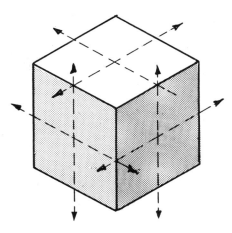

We may have exact or approximate symmetry on a central axis. In two dimensions we were limited to the two possibilities of vertical or horizontal axes. In three, we may have an axis corresponding to all three spatial dimensions. A cube, for example, is symmetrical in plan and in each elevation.

This brings up the distinction between plan and elevation. In architectural and industrial designing, this is significant. Wherever space planning is a major emphasis in the design, the best way of studying the problem is in the plan. The plan itself is a two-dimensional pattern. What it stands for, however, is a system of three-dimensional volumes. In the Beaux Arts tradition great emphasis was placed on formal organization in the plan. One worked with a series of major and minor axes, organizing symmetrical interlocking spaces. Axial balance tended to become an end in itself. Everything was made subservient to the formal values.

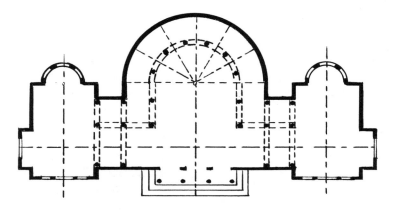

Multiple axes, Beaux Arts planning.

Our own feeling for space planning is much more organic. We determine the size and position of our spaces on the basis of function and circulation. We are, consequently, much less likely to end up with axial schemes.

Radial Balance

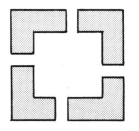

When we discussed radial balance before, we saw that movement around a central point is essential. Its limitations are such that it is chiefly useful for decorative patterns. Consequently, we rarely have much use for this scheme in three-dimensional designing. It occurs occasionally in architectural planning, particularly in the organization of a number of units in space. Its use is pretty specialized, however.

150

Occult balance is by far the most important basic pattern in three-dimensional organization. It is peculiarly suited to the nature of the problem. As stressed before, in occult balance we oppose unlike values, a solid against a space, a strong tone contrast against a weak one. Since the values of our elements are subject to change, depending on the position of the observer, the flexibility of occult balance best fits the complexity of our problem.

There is little else we can say about the problem. If you understand the principle, the rest is up to your innate sensitivity in judging the effect of one value on another.

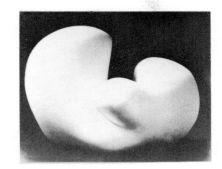

"Human Concretion," by Jean Arp, 1935. (*Courtesy of The Museum of Modern Art.*)

The architect's house, Lincoln, Massachusetts. Walter Bogner, architect. (*Courtesy of the architect. Photograph by Pictorial Services, Inc.*)

151

PROPORTION AND RHYTHM

We have already established the foundation for discussing these two problems. We studied the nature of proportion and rhythm in Chapter 5. We have said enough already about the changing values of plastic elements. What remains is to consider the different aspects of plastic form in which we can express our proportion relationships and our rhythms.

The illustrations under the three following headings demonstrate the possibilities.

Measure relationships between lines, areas, and volumes

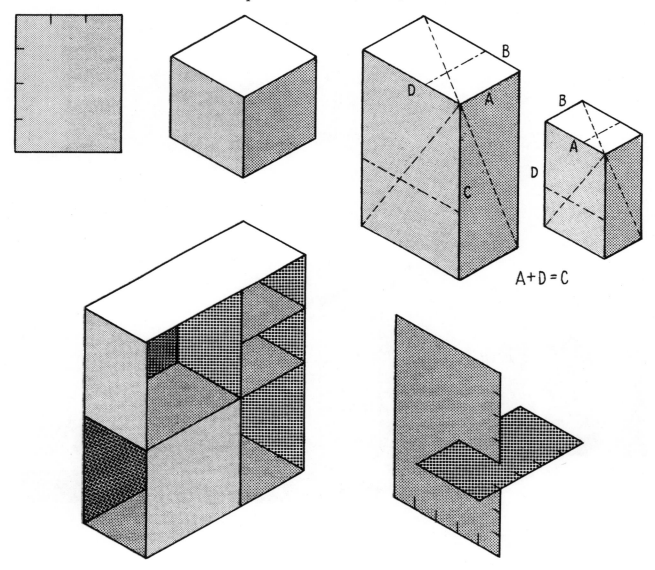

$$A + D = C$$

Tone and textural relationships

Work room, the architect's house, Snake Hill, Belmont, Massachusetts. Carl Koch, architect. (*Courtesy of the architect. Photograph by Pictorial Services, Inc.*)

Dominance and subordination

Koch House, Cambridge, Massachusetts. Edward Stone and Carl Koch, architects. (*Courtesy of the architects. Photograph by Pictorial Services, Inc.*)

153

The chief value of this analysis is to sharpen our perception and to direct our attention to the significant judgments we have to make. No set of rules will make such judgments for us. The only way to mastery in plastic designing, as in two-dimensional designing, is intelligent practice.

VARIETY IN PLASTIC COMPOSITION

Let us review what we said about variety in Chapter 3. We saw in our discussion that there were three sources of variety in a visual pattern:

1. The contrast in visual qualities necessary to give us a formal image introduces variety in the pattern.

2. The different ways in which we can organize the groupings of elements and the movement circuits in our perceptions contribute variety.

3. Absolute variety consists of elements that do not fit into any of the basic rhythms, elements whose function is the same as that of dissonance in music, to enhance the unity by contrast.

To this list we have to add two more sorts of variety to cover the three-dimensional problem:

4. One of these is the often repeated change of value that the plastic elements undergo as we change our own position in relation to them.

5. The other is the plastic quality itself. Since this depends on light as well as on the objective form, it is an ever-changing value. We are so familiar with the changing patterns of light on the objects about us, that we are inclined to take them for granted. It is only when this variety is pointed up by a special presentation, as in the theater, that we respond fully. Nevertheless, it is a valuable resource which we use unconsciously, if not consciously.

MATERIAL, STRUCTURE, AND FORM

Before we leave the problems of three-dimensional form, I should be more specific about one of the themes that has recurred a number of times in our discussion—the way in which material and structure influence form. A few examples will help to make this clear.

Such influences are present even in two-dimensional design. We explicitly or implicitly recognize this in our choice of media, for example. We shall have to handle the same idea quite differently in water color and oil, in pen and lithograph. When we get into three-dimensional, plastic materials, this influence is even more striking. We have spoken repeatedly of the necessity for imagining our form through material, for letting our formal relationships grow out of structural relationships. Let us see how this works.

Homogeneous Materials

The illustration shows two handlings of the same subject by Jules Struppeck. The first composition was done in terra cotta; the raw material, clay. Clay is plastic in the literal sense. That does not mean, however, that any form can be imposed on it. Its very plasticity is a limitation. Until it dries, only a limited volume can be supported without an interior framework. In its own nature, stability of the form requires that the bulk of the mass be within the base of support. Even then, the mass cannot be piled too high without having the weight of the upper part deform the clay underneath. The logical expression of these facts is the cone or the pyramid. If you let a stream of sand fall from your hand, it will pile up into conical form. If you scrape away the edges of the cone at the base to make straight sides, a pyramid will result. The balance between gravity and friction expresses itself in these forms. With clay, the coherence of the mass is much greater than with sand. Nevertheless, the same forces are at work. These limitations are counterbalanced to a degree by using wood or metal armatures to help support the weight.

Even so, in terra-cotta sculpture, from which the armature has to be removed, the nature of clay requires a compact, closed-form treatment. In order to fire the clay, it must be hollow (actually a thin shell with continuous open space penetrating all the volumes). This means that the inside clay and the armature have to be removed when the surface has dried enough to be self-supporting. The forms used have to be imagined within these limitations.

Technically, a terra-cotta figure can be built in two ways. The volumes can be coiled up out of ropes of clay or thrown on a wheel like pieces of ceramic. In this case the forms are light, approximating cylindrical shape. They are made hollow to begin with. They have to be structurally balanced in relation to each other at every point in the building operation. In the other method, the form is built solid, with or without an armature, and hollowed out. In both cases, the form must be imagined within the material and technical limitations.

Two versions of "The Klansmen," by Jules Struppeck.

155

To return to the illustration, notice the conelike enclosing volume of the group. There are no outflung, unsupported forms. Everything is compact. Undercuttings are slight. There are penetrations through the mass, but the separate volumes are contacted and interlocked for stability. Here is a form richly imagined and fully expressive, but one that grows organically out of the nature of clay.

Terra cotta.

"The Klansmen," by Jules Struppeck (1947 and 1948). (*Courtesy of the artist.*)

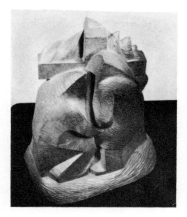

Wood carving.

The group of two kneeling figures, also by Struppeck, illustrated in the preceding chapter, is likewise in terra cotta. The form here is much more open. As we pointed out before, though, cylindrical volumes dominate. We have seen how the cylinder is an organic clay form. The cylinders of legs, arms, and torsos are cleverly interlocked into a stable structure. Hands and feet are tied into bodies or base to leave no unsupported masses. The contrast between this group and "The Klansmen" illustrates the variety of form that can come out of the same set of limitations.

Now contrast the terra-cotta "Klansmen" with the same subject in wood. Here both the material and the technique presented a different set of limitations and expressive potentialities. The operation is not one of building up the form, but of cutting away, of liberating the form visualized in the block. The direction and cutting qualities of the grain were important factors influencing form. Contrast the rounded forms in the terra cotta, approximating cones and cylinders, with the sharply marked planes in the wood carving. These planes, corners, and edges are natural forms in wood. So are the subtle convex and concave movements of the planes. In terra cotta, we can get the latter, but not the former. (Imagine trying to hollow out or coil up these intricate angular volumes, keeping the wall an even thickness.)

Although the idea is the same in both compositions, although their expressive qualities are similar, the whole form and every component part differ because they were projected through different media.

Assembled Materials

When we pass from the problems of forming a continuous, homogeneous material to those of building up a form out of different parts, the necessity of thinking through the material becomes more acute still. We have to be concerned not only with the shape and structure of each part, but with the problem of joining them together structurally. Finally, when we use different materials in the same composition, the achievement of the right form requires a high order of sympathetic understanding and technical knowledge.

This is obviously too complex a subject to cover in detail here. We can analyze the general conditions for solving such problems and then illustrate them.

Three-dimensional forms can be thought of, we said, as a diagram of stresses in material. Each part and each joint is doing some kind of work. If the form has been imagined through material rather than imposed on material, each part is properly shaped and adapted

157

to the work it has to do. A good way of getting at this idea is through mechanics. The basic stresses are compression, tension, torsion, and shear. Compression means the downward pressure of a load on a supporting member. Tension means pull. Torsion means twisting. Shear is defined as the action of a force "that causes or tends to cause two contiguous parts of a solid body to slide on each other."*

Different materials have different capacities to withstand these stresses. The work a member has to do will determine to some degree the material to be used and its shape and size. One part of mechanical engineering is the science of computing the stresses in a structure and of balancing the materials and their joinings to withstand these stresses properly. Architects, for example, must understand the basic engineering principles involved in building. In a complicated problem, engineering specialists have to work in collaboration with the architect to help him project his form through the materials he uses. All designers have to take these structural problems into consideration in shaping their forms.

There is an accumulation of rule-of-thumb practice for common materials. We are all more or less familiar with this guiding tradition. Real imagination is never content to rest with the traditional way, however. It is always re-exploring materials to find new ways of using them, new potential forms that lie hidden in them. The Maillart bridge we discussed in the last chapter is an excellent example of this. Maillart applied the same imaginative understanding of ferroconcrete to the Cement Industries Pavilion for the Swiss Exposition of 1939. This exciting elliptical shell of reinforced concrete, 38 feet high with a 38-foot span, varies from $2\frac{1}{2}$ to $1\frac{3}{4}$ inches in thickness. Here is real structural imagination expressing itself in a form of transcendent beauty.

Plywood is another material that has captured the imagination of contemporary designers. The principle is simple. The growth of wood imparts great strength along the grain. Across the grain, the material is relatively weak. By building up layers in which the grain runs alternately lengthwise and crosswise, much greater strength is achieved. Lamination has been used for centuries. Fine painting panels were made in this way in the Middle Ages. It has remained for contemporary designers to explore the full formal potentialities of the technique. We see it flower into wooden arches of prodigious span or into the new molded forms of Charles Eames's furniture.

* Webster's *Collegiate Dictionary*

Cement Industries Pavilion, Swiss Exposition, Zurich, 1939. Designed by Robert Maillart. (*Courtesy of Dr. Siegfried Giedion. Photograph by H. Wolf-Benders Erben, Zurich.*)

Molded plywood chair. Designed by Charles Eames. (*Courtesy of the designer.*)

159

Part of your job in learning to design is to develop this ability to understand material and to project your imagination through it. Every design problem you undertake is training in this. You can concentrate on the problem, though, by trying to explore freshly any simple material. Paper is a good starting point.

Paper is so familiar that we think we know all there is to know about it. We use it in a hundred ways, usually with little understanding or respect. Really look at it, for a change. Explore its inherent qualities, and discover what forms and techniques can best adapt these qualities to withstand the four basic stresses. For example, how does a flat plane react to compression? How is this reaction changed by curving the plane? Carry this kind of thought on to imaginative applications of structural and plastic expression. Once we begin to think about these questions, a whole new world of form opens up. Our imagination leaps from one new possibility to another.

The illustration shows some of the work my students have done with paper. The same approach can be applied to other materials. This is not an end in itself, although effective use of similar ideas has been made in display, for instance. Its chief value lies in lending wings to our creative imagination, and in developing sympathy for material and a responsible attitude toward the problems of form.

READING LIST

Van Doren, Harold: *Industrial Design*, McGraw-Hill Book Company, Inc., New York, 1940. Chapters 10 and 11.

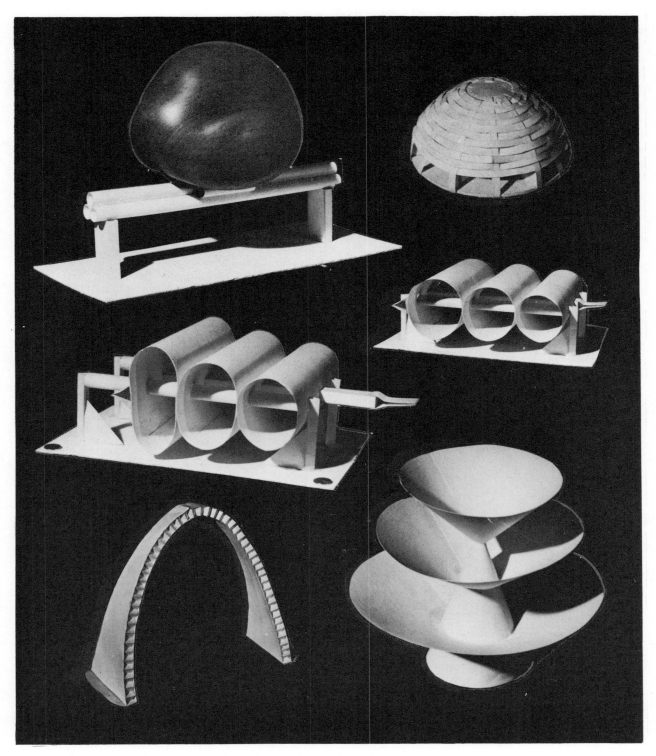

Structural paper work by the author's students, Tulane School of Architecture.

PROBLEM X

Purpose:

To explore further the problems of plastic organization.

Problems:

1. Plastic lines in space. Design and construct an abstract, plastic composition using line and space. The defined spaces should be considered just as material a part of the design as the actual lines. *Keep it simple.*

   Specifications:

   1. Materials:
      Any linear material such as dowels, wire, string, etc. may be used. You can incorporate a base of cardboard or balsa wood or make the design self-supporting.
   2. Presentation:
      a. Consider the characteristics of your different materials. Try to exploit their intrinsic potentialities.
      b. Consider carefully the problems of joining. Work out the joints so that they will be both structurally sound and satisfactory visual elements in the design.
      c. Keep the scale suitable to your materials.

2. Free plastic composition. Design and construct an abstract plastic composition incorporating solids, planes, lines, and space. *Keep it simple.* Beyond the factors already explored, consider particularly in this composition the tone and textural relationships of your different materials.

3. Exploration of the structural and formal possibilities of paper. Using a good grade of detail paper, design and construct a group of paper structures. The following points are suggested as guides:
   a. Explore the potentialities of paper in relation to mechanical stresses:
      Forms for enhanced weight-bearing.
      Forms for enhanced resistance to tension.
      A paper spring.
   b. Can you give the plane of paper the effect of double curvature? Can you make it into a hemisphere, for instance?
   c. Relation between planes and space. By cutting and folding, how can a plane of paper be made to articulate space?
   d. From a 1-foot-square piece, construct the tallest self-supporting tower you can.

4. Arrange and mount your constructions on a sheet of illustration board with titles, diagrams, etc., to explain your work.

12 LIGHT AND MOVEMENT

We have three purposes in this chapter. First, we left a number of loose threads at various points in our previous discussion involving problems of light and movement. Now we can tie them in. Second, an understanding of the effects of light on form and color is an essential part of a designer's experience. Even though he may not use light directly, this knowledge is equally fundamental in two-dimensional design. We shall lay the foundation for this experience here. Third, light and movement are themselves vehicles for designing. Each of these fields in itself affords material for a book. We cannot treat them exhaustively. At the same time, we cannot leave the subject of designing without outlining these exciting potentialities of expression.

Everything we have been studying about the visual side of designing depends finally on light. The fact of light is so commonplace a miracle that we overlook it most of the time. Only when we can use its effect expressively, as in painting, architecture, or light itself, as in the theater, do we consciously consider it. Yet, we must all be sun worshipers in our way. Light is part of the very substance of life. Darkness and death are correlated in our thought and speech.

Actually, the things we design, both in two and in three dimensions, are reflectors to give us the pattern of light we want. In that sense, we have been working with light as a designing medium all through this book. There is another way in which we can use light, not indirectly, but directly. Let us begin to explore this way by listing those arts of design in which light and movement play a dominant part. We made the distinction earlier between physically static arts and the arts with dimensions in time. Most of these, we found, incorporate sound as well as vision. Movies, theater, opera, dance, and so on, are examples. Outside this group is another that involves light or movement or both. Still photography, architectural and interior lighting, display lighting, light modulators, "lumia," and mobile constructions are examples.

We shall proceed to outline the qualities of light as design "materials," and then to suggest the applications using examples from these various fields. Because we are largely dependent on various types of lighting instruments, our discussion will have to be more specifically technical than elsewhere in the book. Our interest is still in the basic principles.

DIMENSIONS OF LIGHT

Tonal Qualities

We are already familiar with the tonal dimensions of light from our study in Chapter 2. To review what we said there, the tonal dimensions of light are:

Brightness: the amount of light. We have to consider this dimension in two respects. We can talk about the absolute brightness of the light source itself, or about the relative brightness of light reflected from surfaces. When we get into the technical problems of light design, the control and measurement of these two aspects of brightness become very important. Here, it is enough to be aware of them.

Hue: the redness, blueness, greenness, and so on, of light. This has to be thought of in the same two ways. We can perceive hue as a direct quality of the light. When we are using colored light on surfaces, though, we have to consider the reflecting powers of the surface as well. If the surface is neutral, this is a simple matter. When the surface is colored, the relationship becomes very complex. There is no satisfactory simple way to systematize this behavior of colored light on colored surfaces. We must have an accurate measurement of the actual wave-length content of the light and of the reflecting power of the surface in order to make dependable judgments. Since we depend in practice largely on color filters such as stage gelatin for coloring light, there is a simple empirical method for determining the effect on pigment. Simply hold the filter be-

164

tween your eyes and the pigments or materials you plan to use. A very close approximation of the light effect will be obtained.

SATURATION: the relative hue purity in the light. We can visualize this dimension as the balance between chromatic and achromatic qualities in our sensation. We must clarify one point here. When we were talking about pigment mixtures, black was a positive achromatic tone. Black mixed with a hue pigment reduced both the value and the intensity. In light, we got the corresponding effect by reducing the brightness. The saturation of the light remains constant. There is just more or less of it. Practically, we have two ways of controlling saturation—we can add achromatic light from another light source, or we can add some of the complementary wave lengths. We do this either by using them in another source or by using one filter that permits some of the complementary wave lengths to pass.

This brings up the question of tone control.

Tone Control

We can control the brightness of the light itself in two ways— either by selecting a light source of the required brightness, or by using some sort of dimmer control.

Hue control offers four possibilities:

FIRST: One way is to use color filters. Colored lamps, or a color screen over the light source, will filter out the wave lengths we do not want. Filters are commonly made of colored glass or gelatin. Since they work by selective transmission, they inevitably cut down the brightness of the light.

SECOND: The neon and fluorescent lights produce a given hue directly. They are, consequently, much more efficient in that you use all of the light instead of wasting part of it. They have the disadvantage that they cannot yet be controlled adequately on dimmer* and they are limited to one type of distribution. We shall discuss distribution in a minute.

THIRD: Color can be controlled by reflection. We can use a colored reflecting screen as a secondary light source. For direct control this is an inefficient device because the reflecting screen absorbs and disperses so much of the light. But it is an important factor in composing light on objects.

* The new cold cathode fluorescent tube can be dimmed down to 10 to 15 per cent of its capacity. At this point the light goes out. If this disadvantage can be overcome to provide continuous dimming, these tubes will be admirable light sources for three-color control of tone.

165

FOURTH: We can use additive mixture to control our hue. This is done by overlapping two or more different-colored lights on a surface. It is the principle behind strip light color control for which we use an instrument made up of a number of small sources of different hue mounted in a single hood. If we have dimmer control over each color, we can get a wide range of hue by varying the proportions of the different colors. We usually use the light primaries: red, green, and blue; or the secondaries: yellow-orange, blue-green, and red-violet, as our basic hues.

Formal Qualities of Light

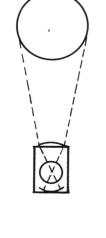

We have to think about this problem from two angles, the pattern of light in space, and the pattern on objects in space. Let us see what we mean by these two ideas.

PATTERNS OF LIGHT IN SPACE

The pattern of light in space depends on three factors. *First*, the distribution of the instrument or instruments we use. The kind of light source, hood, reflectors, and lenses determine this. The problem is too technical to explore in detail, but we can get the essential idea by the following discussion of three typical patterns of light distribution.

LENS UNITS, such as spotlights, give us a long, sharply defined cylinder of light in space. It has the characteristic of nearly uniform brightness in cross section. Because the rays of light are almost parallel, brightness does not fall off as much with distance as it does in the other two distributions. There is a sharp edge to the volume of light.

FLOOD UNITS give us a wider distribution but a less positive form. They consist of an open hood, with or without reflector, and a light source. The actual shape of the distribution depends on the shape of the hood and reflector. There is more variation in brightness in different parts of the distribution. Brightness falls off more sharply with distance. The edge of the light volume is still positive, but softer than in a spotlight.

STRIP UNITS give us a wide, fan-shaped distribution. Because they use multiple sources or a linear source, as in fluorescent tubes, the light is relatively shadowless.

166

Second, another factor that determines the form of light in space is the way we combine the distributions of two or more instruments. The inherent shape of the individual light volumes plus the directions from which they come are our variables.

Third, the balance of brightness, hue, and saturation in the pattern has its effect. It is like the pattern of pigments on a surface, but here we are dealing with brighter or dimmer volumes of space, or with different-colored volumes.

PATTERNS OF LIGHT ON OBJECTS IN SPACE

The form of light in space is not revealed to us directly. It is only under special conditions that we are even aware of it, as when we see a powerful searchlight at night or a beam of light in dusty or smoky atmosphere. We see the effect of this form only when it strikes objects in space. The reason for discussing the form in space is that it helps us to understand the effect of light on objects. We can get at this best by breaking down the problem into characteristic relationships between a single spotlight and a plane in space.

We will begin with a stationary spotlight and see the effect of changing the angle of a plane in relation to it. If we place a flat plane at right angles to the axis of the light, we get a maximum even brightness over the whole surface. As we turn the plane away from this position in any direction, the light falls more obliquely along the surface. Less light strikes the surface and brightness decreases. With large planes, the inverse-square law makes itself felt. (Brightness is inversely proportional to the distance from the source.) The spot directed obliquely along the surface of a wall, for example, results in a gradation of brightness. The part nearest the light is brighter. As the plane moves away from the light, the brightness falls off. At the corner, where the adjoining wall faces the light, the brightness jumps up again.

At right angles to the light axis.

At an oblique angle to the light axis.

Parallel and at right angles to the light axis.

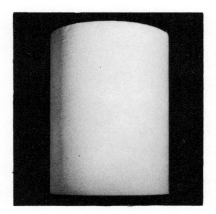

Gradation on curved plane.

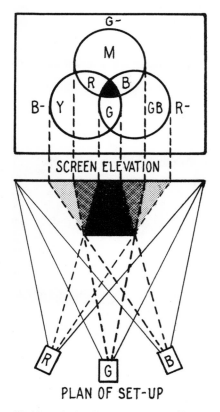

PLAN OF SET-UP

Half and absolute shadows. (Diagrammatic analysis of color modulator, Plate VII, page 99.)

When we use a curved plane, another characteristic pattern results. We get a double gradation of tone. The form is brightest where the surface is at right angles to the axis of the light. The brightness falls off in both directions from this point. The edges at which the plane turns out of the light will be definite, but the line is soft rather than sharp.

When we start to put these different characteristic light-plane patterns together, the possibilities are endless. We can contrast the effects of flat and curved planes. We can build gradations, alternations, similarities of shape, size, position, tone, and so on. The next step is to amplify the pattern of light in space by using more than one instrument or different kinds of instruments to play with different colors and brightnesses.

This introduces three new factors:

1. Cast Shadows.
2. Translucency.
3. Reflections.

CAST SHADOWS

Cast shadows can become a very important element in our composition. We saw in Chapter 9 how they can be used to define form. They can also add new formal and tonal elements for us to work with. One of the most fascinating possibilities in this respect results from the building up of tones in the shadows by simultaneous contrast. You can get a surprising range of subtle color effects by using just one hue and an achromatic light. Let us see how this works. Whenever you have more than one source, your cast shadows have two or more values. First, there are shadows that do not receive light from one source but do from the other. Second, there are absolute shadows, receiving light from neither source. Those lighted from one side are much more positive in giving induced colors than the absolute shadows are. When you use two or more colored sources, these half and full shadows result in an amazing range of tonal mixtures. The diagram shows the underlying principle, using the three light primaries. Three spotlights have been focused on a plane. The free-form shape has been suspended in front of them. Where it cuts off the light from one source, we get the additive secondary mixture from the other two lights. Where two sources are blocked, we have the straight primary color of the third. Where the shadow is absolute, we have black: that is, a complete absence of light.

168

TRANSLUCENCY AND TRANSPARENCY

If we use materials that are not fully opaque, a new range of possibilities opens up. The effect of light coming through the surfaces is fascinating. It has two values, the effect on the translucent surface itself, and the spill on surrounding surfaces. A somewhat similar but more positive effect is possible if we use a transparent area or hole through an opaque form. The light travels through the hole giving us positive light-and-shadow patterns.

REFLECTION

Reflection is the third factor to be considered. The reflecting character of the surface is important here. This varies from a general diffused reflection from mat surfaces to regular reflection from mirror surfaces. The effect will range from a softening glow of reflected light in shadow areas to the reflection of the light source itself. Here, particularly, we have to take into consideration the tone of the areas. It will qualify the color of the light it reflects. The study of this phenomenon is of great value for painting.

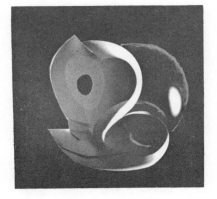

Light modulator by one of the author's students, Newcomb College.

MOVEMENT IN LIGHT

Finally, we have to think about movement in our pattern. This may be of two kinds. First, there may be actual physical movement, either in the form or in the light. Movement in the light is likely to produce an effect of physical movement in the form as well. Second, a change in any of the qualities of the light will result in an effect of movement.

Now we must think about the different ways in which we can use light as a designing medium.

LIGHT AS A DESIGNING MEDIUM

Photography

The camera is an instrument for recording the effect of light on surfaces. It can be used in many ways. Usually we are probably more interested in other factors than in the light pattern itself. We can use the camera, however, as a tool for giving our light designs a permanent form.

169

The simplest step in this direction is the *photogram*. It is a direct recording of a light pattern on sensitized paper without the aid of a camera. The light is controlled by masks and by length of exposure to build a pattern of shapes in different values. It is a fascinating technique in itself. It has been used effectively in advertising illustration.

Where the camera is used, we do the basic designing with light and with the objects on which the light falls. The camera records and gives permanent form to the pattern. But it requires specialized technical skill to use the camera. The nature and limitations of the instrument make demands on the designing of the light pattern. You have to know what the camera can do and design your light within these limitations. Moviemaking is a good example of that fact.

Photogram, work of the Photography Course, Newcomb College.

Movie, Stage, and Display Lighting

These fields offer rich possibilities for the creative use of light. Particularly in display lighting, the surface has only been scratched. The "cake of custom" is very strong. We still depend largely on obvious devices and tried clichés. Take the question of electric signs, for example. The old pattern of an elaborate layout delineated with small incandescent lamps has been largely displaced by neon tubing, with or without movement. Our solution in both cases has

Stage setting for "Chanticleer," by the author, 1934. Lighting by Stanley McCandless, Department of Drama, Yale University. (*Photograph by Morris Shapiro.*)

170

been the first and obvious answer. We have only begun to explore the possibilities of indirect and reflected light, of light-transmitting materials such as lucite, of translucency and transparency. A wealth of possibilities with subtleties of expression far more effective than our present blatant pattern awaits exploration.

In the field of movie and stage lighting, our understanding of the potentialities is much more advanced. We have developed both a more adequate set of specialized instruments and means for their control. From Linnebach and Belasco to the present time there has been a steady progression of developing resources and of understanding in using them creatively.

Architectural and Interior Lighting

The development of stage lighting presents a lesson that is important here as well. Design in light is at least as much a question of developing instruments for special functions as it is of the way we use our instruments. A realization of this truth has accounted for the great strides we have made in recent years in lighting the outsides and insides of buildings. Illuminating engineers have made careful studies of the amounts and kinds of light required for the best performance of different tasks. They have designed new instruments to provide these qualities. The functional side of lighting has made great progress, but we still have a long way to go, both in function and in expression.

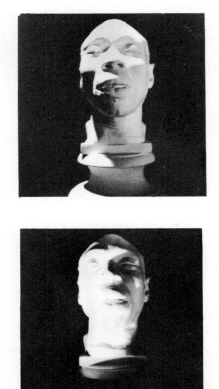

This is quite evident in much exterior lighting. Until recently, buildings designed as modulators for sunlight have been lighted at night in a completely fortuitous fashion. A couple of floodlights have been turned on them, or some similar crude device employed, with disastrous results. The forms, conceived in terms of light from above, have disintegrated when lighted from below. The charming old Bulfinch State House in Boston with its central colonnade and focal gold dome is a satisfying design of its time. A number of years ago someone got the idea that it ought to be lighted at night. They stuck two floodlights with amber filters behind the colonnade, one on either side. The result gave the impression that the building was on fire. The juke-box quality completely distorted the rhythm and unity of the composition. To waive the question of taste, the point is that architectural forms, interior as well as exterior, have to be designed as parts of a light pattern. We do this traditionally with reference to the sun. Cornices, moldings, string courses, and so forth, from classical times on, are actually light modulators. The use of artificial night lighting introduces new problems. The form has to be adapted to both kinds of light sources.

Effect of direction on the appearance of a plastic form.

171

Frank Lloyd Wright's Johnson's Wax Company building at Racine, Wisconsin, is a beautiful example of perceptive and imaginative handling. The continuous band of glass tubing around the building serves a double function. It admits daylight to the interior in a controlled pattern and serves as a focal accent in the exterior composition. At night, the fluorescent tubing built into it lights the interior in the same controlled pattern. It also serves the same accenting function in the exterior appearance. Here is a real light-form composition.

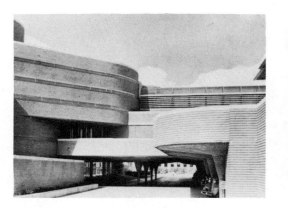 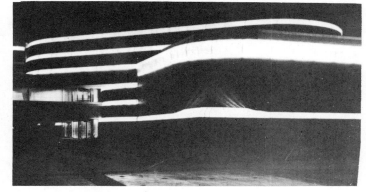

The Johnson's Wax Company, Racine, Wisconsin. Frank Lloyd Wright, architect. (*Courtesy of the architect. Photograph courtesy of Johnson's Wax.*)

Light Modulators

Light modulators are abstract plastic compositions in light on forms in space. They are valuable devices for exploring the problems of light design. They also have a direct expressive value in themselves, like a painting or a piece of sculpture. Our analysis of the relationships of a light source and a plane in space provides a basis for this sort of exploration. It is very important at the start to work with simple forms and only one or two instruments. The possibilities are so fascinating that it is easy to lose one's way in open-mouthed wonder. This may be fun, but it does not prove much. If you work at first with means simple enough to keep under control, you will build up a background of experience which will enable you to tackle more complex problems with assurance. The illustrations show some of the compositions made by my students at Newcomb College.

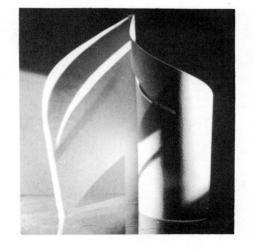

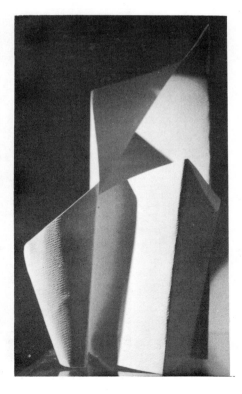

Light modulators by the author's students, Newcomb College.

"Lumia": The Art of Mobile Light

"*Lumia*" is a name coined by Thomas Wilfred for design in moving patterns of light projected on a translucent screen. It is sometimes called "color music," rather unfortunately, it seems to me. The problem does have one point in common with music or the dance. It involves a design in time. Music is sometimes used as accompaniment or "lumia" used to accompany music. There is no harm in this. The design, however, is a purely visual pattern and "music" gives it a misleading connotation. The basic principle is the control of the form, color, and movement of light patterns on the screen. Wilfred has developed a "color organ," really a very complex control board, which gives him command over his instruments. All the possibilities of reflection, refraction, pattern projection, and so forth, are made use of. In a developed form, "lumia" constitutes a highly technical problem in light engineering. But anyone with a few spotlights and dimmers can construct a translucent screen and experiment with these fascinating possibilities.

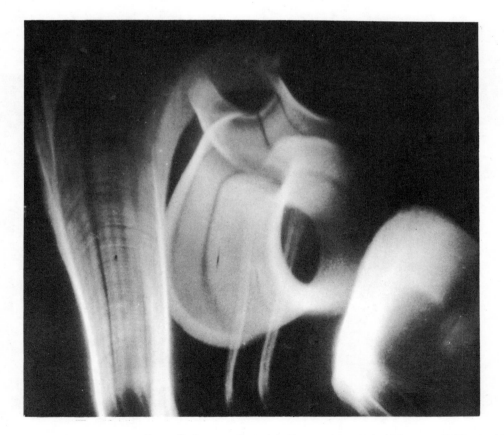

"Passage from a 'Lumia' Composition," by Thomas Wilfred. (*Courtesy of the Art Institute of Light, West Nyack, New York.*)

174

DESIGN IN MOVEMENT

As we saw in Chapter 4, movement, in a subjective sense, is an intrinsic part of all visual design. It is one of our main expressive resources. Nor should these facts be at all strange. If light is a part of the substance of life, movement is of its essence. Time and change, the two essentials of movement, are dimensions of living.

They are also objective dimensions of one group of visual arts—movies, theater, and dance in particular. In this book, since we are concerned only with the fundamentals of designing, we obviously cannot go very far with the specific problems of movement as they apply to these fields. But we can survey the dimensions of physical movement itself, the dimensions in which we express the pattern of our designs.

The Dimensions of Movement

DIRECTION

The first distinguishing characteristic of movement is its direction. This may be continuous in one direction. It may involve change of direction. The change may be one of regular progression or of opposition. Each of these possibilities has its own expressive character.

RATE

A second dimension of movement is rate. It may be fast or slow or any intermediate speed. The rate can be constant, or it can change in regular progression or abruptly. These changes can themselves be patterned into larger rhythms. Rate, of course, has a pronounced expressive value.

KIND

Movements can also be characterized as to kind. They may be continuous in a given direction, linear or rotary. They can be periodic, like the swing of a pendulum.

FORM

When we begin to organize movements together in time, certain patterns will result that have a recognizable form character. They are like themes in music. Let us take a simple example. Suppose we suspend two pendulums of different lengths from the same support. If we start them out together, an interesting thing happens. The shorter pendulum swings faster than the longer one does. It will quickly get out of step with the slower pendulum. As they swing, though, they will come into phase again, only to lose it. We immediately recognize the formal pattern of this fluctuation in phase. This example illustrates two kinds of form in movement. The simple pattern of the pendulum itself is one. The building up and loss of phase between the two is another. These forms can become very complex as we pattern different movements together. The same sort of thing happens in dancing, where two or more groups are played against each other in different rhythms.

Effect of Movement on Form

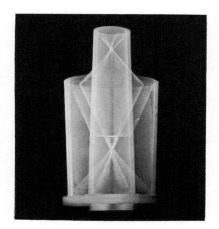

Virtual volume through movement.

A very interesting and significant aspect of the movement problem is the effect movement has on our perception of form. I am not competent to make a full analysis of this effect. That would pertain more to psychology than to design, in any event. It is enough that we are aware of the possibility. Two examples will illustrate what I mean. Suppose we paint a figure eight on a circular disk that can be revolved. As the pattern starts rotating, it acquires a startling elasticity. The figure itself seems to wriggle in a sort of amoeboid fashion. The other example is even more significant for mobile composition. We will insert a dowel in the edge of a horizontal turntable. As the table revolves, the movement of the dowel will circumscribe a cylindrical volume of space. We perceive this volume as a definite thing. It is a *virtual volume*. Many mobile compositions play with this idea of virtual volumes. They can be concrete enough to photograph, as the illustration shows.

Mobile Composition

The movies and the dance are perhaps the two most familiar visual arts with strong composed movement. Movies usually involve a dominant storytelling emphasis. (So may the dance, but it is usually more abstract.) Nevertheless, the time sequence is of basic importance. The more abstract films bring this out clearly. There are wonderful unexplored possibilities here.

A number of contemporary artists have experimented with abstract mobile sculpture. One thinks particularly of Alexander Calder. This sort of thing is again an excellent training ground for understanding the problems of movement. It is also a valid kind of expression in its own right.

We have been able to do no more than scratch the surface of two exciting fields in this chapter. They are fields that are still almost virgin in spite of the work that has been done. Both in their relation

176

to the more conventional arts and in their own right they offer us
new and untried possibilities.

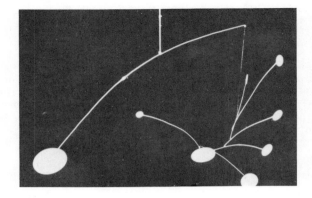

Hanging Mobile, by Alexander Calder.
(*Courtesy of Mrs. Meric Gallery. Photograph by Herbert Matter.*)

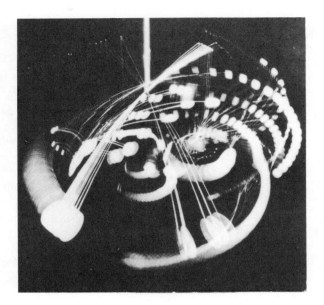

Mobile in action. (*Photograph by Herbert Matter.*)

READING LIST

Kepes, Gyorgy: *The Language of Vision*, P. Theobald, Chicago, 1944.
Section on Light and Color.

Moholy-Nagy, L: *Vision in Motion*, P. Theobald, Chicago, 1947. Space-Time Problems and Motion Picture.

PROBLEM XI

Purpose:

To get an introduction to the design possibilities of light and movement.

Problems:

1. Light modulator with one source. Design and construct a simple plastic composition to pattern light from a single source. Do not make a form and then try to light it. Decide on the direction of the light (front, side, above, below, on a level). Then build your form in the light, bending, folding, cutting, etc. to make your composition.

Specifications:

1. Materials:

   a. Build the modulator out of white Bristol board. It should be stiff enough to be self-supporting, but flexible enough to bend without cracking.
   b. Fasten your pieces where necessary with paper clips or glue.
   c. A small baby spotlight, such as is used for photographic purposes or window display, makes an excellent instrument to work with. Lacking this, an ordinary gooseneck desk lamp will serve. A dimmer is desirable to control brightness. A small Variac dimmer is excellent if available. If you do not have one, you can still work with the form characteristics.

2. Light modulator with two sources. Design and construct a simple plastic composition to pattern light from two sources. Use two instruments from different directions. If you have no dimmer, place your instruments at different distances from the modulator to control relative brightness. Proceed as before.

   An interesting variation on this problem is to use a colored gelatin over one of the lights. This gives you a wide range of subtle hue effects, since complementary tones are induced in the half shadows.

3. Light modulator with movement. (This problem is practical only if you have at least two dimmers). Design and construct a plastic light composition in time. For this you will need three spotlights, preferably three dimmers, and colored gelatins. Work out a composition in which the light pattern changes. The pattern of change, too, should be designed. You can do this by forming the modulator to give several different patterns under different lights and combinations of lights. Then work out the sequence of change by bringing the lights on and off with your dimmers. Consider the rate of change; the kind, whether continuous or reversing; etc.

4. Mobile sculpture. Design and construct a simple plastic composition incorporating physical movement. This does not mean merely something that will move, like a jack-in-the-box. The movement should be incorporated as an integral part of the composition. It should itself have form.

13 DESIGN IN ACTION: Designing This Book

The study of designing presents us with a dilemma. Visual relations can be generalized. Structural relations are always specific. We have our choice of studying actual cases of designing, in which the organic connection between visual and structural relationships is clear, or of concentrating on the general nature of visual relations. In the one case, we deal with the whole problem of designing, but sacrifice breadth of application. In the other, we run the risk of false emphasis on formal problems.

I have chosen the latter attack for the body of this book, hoping to get around the weakness of such an attack through the designing you have done for the problems accompanying each chapter. Through that practice you have re-established in your experience the organic unity of the design process. This, I hope, will have corrected the necessarily biased emphasis of the text. In this final chapter, I shall adopt the other alternative. I shall use the designing of this book to draw together the various factors we have examined in isolation and to relate them to the causal factors of purpose, materials, and technique. In conclusion, we shall share this one example of the organic unity of designing in action.

NATURE OF THE PROBLEM

The first thing about any design problem is its specific nature. Designing this book has aspects in common with book design generally. But we can get at those common problems only through the specific nature of this one body of material. For instance, every book design has two aspects. We must consider the organization and expression of the ideas it is to contain. We must also consider the physical form in which these ideas are to be presented. The first problem is the content; the second is the material book. The causal factors of purpose, form, material, and technique apply to both. This is true of all books, but we can never really get at these problems abstractly. They can be fully grasped only in their context.

FIRST CAUSE: Growth of the Idea

I think we can define the purpose of this book best by considering how the idea for it grew. I first approached the problem of teaching design fundamentals (not a limited application of designing, but the basic principles specific to all design) in a course given at Harvard by Professor Robert D. Feild and myself jointly. Any undertaking of this kind is inevitably indebted to the pioneering work of the Bauhaus. At Harvard, we had the great privilege of help and encouragement from Walter Gropius. Josef Albers, of the Bauhaus and Black Mountain College, gave periodic seminars in connection with the course. These contacts were invaluable to me. Professor Albers's method of teaching, particularly, opened a new realm of experience to me.

This was all background, but as yet there was no thought of a book. It was not until I came to Newcomb College that the idea began to take form. It germinated from a series of wall charts I made to accompany my class problems. One of the discouragements every teacher meets is that students retain so little information from lectures, demonstrations, and reading. This is not a criticism

Wall chart by the author.

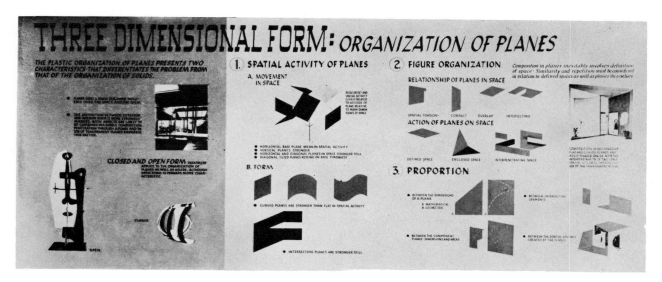

of students, merely a limitation of the learning process. I thought that a visual outline of the material under consideration posted in the workroom might help.

Following out this idea, I made a series of wall charts using diagrams, illustrations, and outline text. I organized the material not merely for illustrative value but to give a visual picture of the design relationships involved. As these charts developed and proved their value in the course, I decided they might be worth publishing. The first conception of the book was simply that, to reproduce the charts with a short accompanying text.

I was so busy keeping one chart ahead of the course that there was no time to do more with the idea until summer vacation. In preparation, I had the charts photographed. I then began work on a text to accompany them. It was very soon apparent that the idea in this form was unsatisfactory. There were two serious flaws in it. First, the text was completely divorced from the illustrations. The visual structure of design relations I felt to be so important was present in the charts, but there was no way for carrying this over into the text. Second, knowing the high cost of publishing, I first visualized the whole chart made up as one printing plate for photo offset. The photographs demonstrated that there was too wide a range in the character of the material included in the charts for satisfactory reproduction. Making a separate plate for each item would have been the only way to get quality reproduction. This would defeat the intended economy.

From this work, however, a clear conception of the book had gradually evolved. The organization of the idea content had been worked over in course presentation and had been disciplined into visual form in the charts. From the latter came the idea of making the illustrations more than a mere demonstration of the text. Taken with the section headings, they were to provide a visual outline of the whole content of the book. This, then, was the program as it finally evolved:

1. The clear presentation of the complex problems of designing, using the psychology of perception as a structural principle for organizing the material.

2. The visual presentation of this material to accompany the text directly, and to provide an illustrated outline of the whole book.

3. The use of section headings in the dual function of identifying the textual divisions and completing the visual outline.

4. The use of the book itself as an illustration of designing in action. This meant organizing, designing, and producing the book as well as possible. It must be as worthy of the high concept of designing presented in the text as it could be made.

FORMAL CAUSE

This conception immediately suggested certain things about the form of the book:

1. A way had to be worked out for visualizing the structure of the section headings. It should show the main and subordinate divisions of the material. This could be done in standard outline form. The resources of typography and layout suggested an alternative. One could show the same structure by the selection of different sizes and faces of type and by the way one used them in the layout.

Here is an excellent illustration of the way a formal concept is influenced by material and technical potentialities. Between these two alternatives, I felt that the latter offered much more possibility for visual distinction and variety. It was along these lines, consequently, that I let my imagination play.

2. The objective of always keeping text and illustrations united had direct bearing on the book's form. To be practical, a fairly large format was necessary. The principle of layout had to lend itself organically to such treatment.

Thinking along these lines, I saw that a more specific visualization of the probable physical form of the book would be helpful in the writing stage. It would simplify things later to have a fairly clear picture of the relation between text and illustration as I went along. Particularly would this be true for the color illustrations. It was clear to me from the start that I would need more of them than a text can normally afford. These considerations urgently demanded thought from the beginning so that the writing and organization could help to solve them.

You can see how the nature of my problem had led me into a situation that was decidedly out of the ordinary. An author is not normally so intimately concerned with the visual form of his book as this. His responsibility is the writing and the selection of the illustration material. He may have ideas about the visual form, but the publisher usually works them out. I knew a bit about typography and layout, but I lacked professional experience in book designing and production. Still, my problem was such that form and idea could not be separated. Realizing that whatever I did would be in the nature of suggestion rather than a final solution, I could see no way of presenting my material except a provisional layout.

FIRST VISUALIZATION

Logically, it would be desirable to discuss the material and technical causes separately. Concretely, however, they are so intimately related to the development of the formal concept that it will be more meaningful to weave them in as we go along.

My next step, therefore, was to make a tentative decision on the format and on a principle for page layout. In printing, a sequence of pages, usually in multiples of eight, is run through the press on a single large sheet. It takes two runs for black and white, one for each side. Color halftones require a separate run for each color. For binding purposes, these sheets are folded into signatures and the sequence of signatures sewn together as a unit. The exact arrangement of the pages on the printing sheet and the number of pages per signature is a highly technical problem. It depends on the press, folding apparatus, and binding machine to be used. It was obviously impossible, therefore, to determine the exact production procedure at this point. At the same time I had to keep the goal of economic production in mind, and I had to have a relatively large page to make my idea of relating text and illustration practical. From my reading I learned that sizes larger than 8½ by 11 inches cannot in many binderies be bound automatically. They run into more or less hand work, which would, of course, very materially increase production cost. The 8½- by 11-inch format, therefore, seemed the best choice.

The next problem was to decide how to relate the text and illustrations on the page. I knew from my experience in making the charts that I would use a large number of diagrams. Most of these could be relatively small without losing their effectiveness. Of the remaining material, there was a considerable variation in effective scale. Some of the illustrations needed to be large. Others would carry equally well at smaller scale. From this it followed that whatever plan I adopted should afford flexibility. A second consideration had to do with the form of the text. It must be as legible and as distinguished in appearance as possible. Since the choice of type face and point size would determine the amount of copy I could fit into a given space, and since the "weight" of the body type on the page would affect the handling of each page, it seemed desirable to have a specific choice of type in mind as I worked. This is another instance of the reciprocal relation between form and material. I wanted a face neither too light nor too black as a good foil to the illustrations and one that combined legibility with distinction and a contemporary expression. The latter consideration excluded a number of otherwise logical choices. As a tentative selection, I finally determined on a linotype Scotch Modern in twelve-point size leaded two points. This meant that the body size of the type was approximately 12/72 of an inch deep with 2/72 of an inch extra space allowed between lines. The effect of this type in my samples was easily legible with a tone, a dignity, and a clarity I liked.

I could now try for a first approximation of the standard page

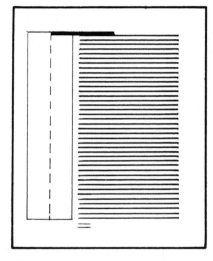

First working out of the skeleton structure for the layout.

layout. Two considerations tended in the direction of an asymmetrical arrangement. By using a larger outside margin, I should have room for small diagrams and illustrations opposite the text. Secondly, there is an optimum length of line for easy readability. I used the rule of thumb that the length of line should fall between one and a half and two alphabets, counting letters, punctuation, and space between words as characters. The length of a line of type is measured in picas (approximately $\frac{1}{6}$ of an inch). I proceeded to count the number of characters in eight or ten lines of my type sample to determine the average number that would fit in a given length. Balancing these variables against each other, I arrived at a line of 26 picas with an average of fifty-nine characters per line. This meant a line approximately $4\frac{1}{3}$ inches long. It is necessary to give these dimensions as approximations since the actual type measure is incommensurate with the inch. For accurate layout work, it is necessary to use a pica rule or, in newspaper work, an agate rule. It is clearer here to approximate the dimensions in inches. I placed this to the inside of the page format, allowing a 3-inch outside margin. This would permit a marginal illustration 2 inches wide with adequate margin space. The depth of the copy was determined to give a good shape to the block of text on the page with top and bottom margins visually related to the vertical margins. This worked out to provide forty-three lines per column.

This description of the layout plan may sound as if the process was determined by purely functional considerations. This is far from the case, if the word "functional" is limited to strictly utilitarian matters. We are always working for a satisfying visual composition in which the tone and texture of the type, the illustrations, and the white space are effectively related. This is hardly a unique problem. Like the design of letters themselves, the possible forms of a page layout are pretty well explored. Again like letter forms, effective page layout fits into a well-established tradition. In its essentials the plan I have outlined closely approximates forms used in medieval manuscripts or Renaissance typography as well as many contemporary designs. In this sense it is not a new invention. It is rather that the functional considerations suggested a certain type of formal solution. Familiarity with tradition automatically enters the designing by influencing our judgments as we work out the balance of factors with which we deal. This is only another way of saying that page layout is not a primary field for designing. Because of well-established reading habits, we are not free to run the printing vertically or backwards. The whole idea is to make the reading process as easy and clear as possible. For that very reason the accepted patterns for page layout are best. Within such a pattern there is ample scope for creative expression in the effectiveness with which it is handled.

184

I now had a definite form for the page. I could use it as a mental picture in considering how to relate text and illustrations as I proceeded with the writing.

WRITING AND VISUALIZING

While still thinking of the charts as illustrations, I had completed a draft of about a third of the text. I commenced to rework this material. The introductory chapter, having only two illustrations, presented no great problem of layout. The paging of subsequent chapters, however, would depend on the space the introduction took. Besides, I was eager to see how the plan would work out. Therefore I began the first dummy layout.

For this rough visualization, I chose half scale as a convenient and economical size. I carefully laid out a double-page spread, ruling the type lines and margins in ink. Over this I placed tracing paper on which the layout could be developed page by page in pencil.

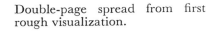

Double-page spread from first rough visualization.

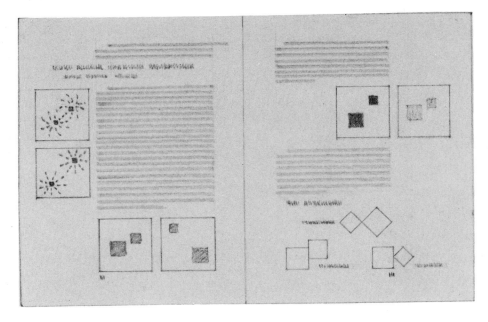

Two new technical problems developed at this point. First, I had to know on which page of the first signature the text would begin. Different publishers use varying organizations for the half title, title page, copyright, dedication, preface, and table of contents. While I could not, therefore, make any final determination, all these items had to be provided for. I examined a number of books the layout of which I admired, and patterned my solution on them. It is standard form for the text to begin on a right-hand page. This worked out to be page 11. Interestingly, when the book was accepted for publication, although my original sequence was changed, the amount of space allotted for these opening pages remained the same. Here was an instance of the way accepted practice in book designing had specific bearing on my particular problem.

Secondly, I had to estimate as accurately as possible the number of characters in the copy to be set. Since I already knew my average number of characters per line of type would be fifty-nine, this problem was easily solved by setting the typewriter for a line of the same length. This made it possible merely to count the lines in the typescript and transfer their number to the layout directly. I could do this only because the format and layout were already determined.

It was exciting to test the planning up to this point. I laid out the first chapter in the determined framework. It was not bad. Many difficulties would arise later. So far, however, the form was realizing my purpose of clarity, flexibility, and distinction.

Each chapter was worked up in this way as it was written, writing and visualizing being carried along together. Chapter 2 introduced another major technical problem, one we have already considered in general. That was the problem of color. I knew the essential illustrations would be an expensive item in the cost of the book. I planned from the first, therefore, to limit color to those illustrations essential to a clear understanding of the text. They were all to be concentrated as much as possible and to be confined to as few signatures as I could manage. The definition of tonal contrast was the first place where the color could not be avoided. This section of text, consequently, had to fall on one page so that the five diagrams could be made on one plate. This sort of problem occurred repeatedly. In the color chapters particularly, it required great care to work out a solution. Visualizing the layout along with the writing was a great help here. In some places the amount of space available for text was determined by the sequence of possible places for illustrations. This frequently meant that the text had to be as concise as possible. Occasionally, I felt as if I were composing a fifty-word telegram.

At first thought, this condition may seem an intolerable limitation. Actually, it is not. I am sure my writing gained rather than lost by the enforced economy. This is an excellent example of the function of limitations in designing. The most difficult problem is that in which we have no limitations. There is no focusing of the possibilities, no point of departure. We can do anything. Therefore frequently we can do nothing. We are frustrated by infinity. It is only when the problem imposes or we arbitrarily set up a limiting field that the directions for liberating our creative imagination become apparent. In the same way, the restrictions of the sonnet or sonata forms are actually not restrictions. They are ready-made fields with recognizable attributes of form within which creative imagination is liberated because it has fixed points of reference to work from. This is a hard truth for beginning designers to accept. It is a welcome truth of creative maturity.

As the book worked out, my original plan of distributing the color through the text proved impossible. What I have said is still valid even though economic considerations forced a different solution. The confirmation of this is the fact that long and careful search failed to find a more economical solution within the framework of using the illustrations to accompany the text.

A similar, though less extreme limitation came from the problems of platemaking. For maximum effectiveness in offset reproduction, where a whole page is made up as one printing plate, it is desirable to keep a reasonable uniformity in the character of the material to be reproduced. This means that illustrations with subtle contrast and others with bold contrast on the same plate cannot be handled with fidelity to both. It also means that line cuts and halftones can be more economically reproduced when not combined on the same plate. These facts influenced my choice of a transparent film printed with various halftone patterns for halftone effects in some of the diagrams. These commercial films make possible a range of halftone effects without the necessity of screening the plates. In a few cases, it was impossible to avoid the combination of halftone and line material, but such combinations were kept to a minimum.

PAGE COMPOSITION

The composition of the individual page layouts was, for the most part, a simple matter. I had determined the principle. The problem was that of fitting the text and illustrations into the pages for best effect. The chief difficulty was to keep the section of text and the illustrations dealing with one subject clearly organized in relation to the page sequence. It would not do, for instance, to have a heading come at the bottom of a right-hand page where it would be divorced from the body of the section on the following spread. The solution of this problem required some expansion and condensation in places. This was done both in the writing and in the size and position of the illustrations.

There were a number of guiding ideas I kept in mind. I tried always to consider the two facing pages as a unit. My illustrations were selected with regard to their value as attractions in the unit composition as well as for their specific point. I have a prejudice against bled illustrations—that is, illustrations that run off the edges of the page. In one place, this was disregarded where it was essential to have the maximum size for the illustration. My feeling on this is admittedly personal. One can find good arguments either way. I happen to like the insulation and unity a good margin gives a page.

One final point. This problem of page layout in relation to the design of the book as a whole is representative of a typical class of design problems. The architect or costume designer for the stage meets it. I mean simply that some designs must be carried out on several different levels at the same time. The page is a unit. It is also part of a double-page spread. The sequence of these units builds up into chapters and ultimately into the book itself. One must consider each level of design for its restricted, but also for its wider, value.

An architect works with his plan, with the interior space, and with the exterior form of his building. Each room is an entity, and a part of a larger pattern. A costume designer must create effective individual costumes, indicative of the character and circumstances of the dramatic personages. At the same time, these units build into scenes and the scenes into acts, ultimately into one visual element of the design of the play as a whole.

With the book, then, each page is a composition and also a part of a larger composition. The unity of the principle of layout serves to tie the whole together, but the whole will be more than a mere sum of the individual pages.

PRESENTATION DUMMY

I had now reached a point in the development of the book at which the content and the visual presentation were established, at least provisionally. The next step was the presentation.

This represents another characteristic aspect of certain kinds of design problems. A painter can go ahead with his work in the dual capacity of creator and critic from blank canvas to framed picture. An architect, an industrial designer, and the author of a book must present their ideas for the approval of the client or publisher before those ideas can be realized in their final form. When you are dealing with this kind of problem, you must have a clear awareness that the presentation is not itself the expression of the idea. It is an in-between step that allows someone else to understand and evaluate. As such, it must do justice to the idea. It must be well done. At the same time, well done implies subservience to its purpose. It is easy, in an architectural rendering, for instance, to overdramatize. A flashy rendering can falsify the real architectural idea; it can actually conceal the lack of such an idea, at least to the uninitiated. One sort of skill, that of making an effective rendering, is substituted for the creative solution of the real problem. Presentation, therefore, is an art in itself. A poor presentation can prejudice the sympathetic consideration of even the best idea. On the other hand, the most attractive presentation will be equally poor in a deeper sense if it does not grow out of the needs of the idea to be presented.

With this book, the presentation dummy is much closer to the actual form of the idea than a blueprint or rendering of a building is. Nevertheless, the presentation problem was essentially the same. All the way through, I had to think in terms of type and reproduction techniques. I had to represent the text and illustrations effectively, but without falsification.

This dummy was made full scale with all the space relations accurately shown. It was made up in sixteen-page signatures as nearly as possible exactly as the material would fit into the printed pages. The photographic illustrations were made to scale to fit their determined places in the layout. Diagrams and text were indicated in pencil. Color diagrams were rendered in color. I made no at-

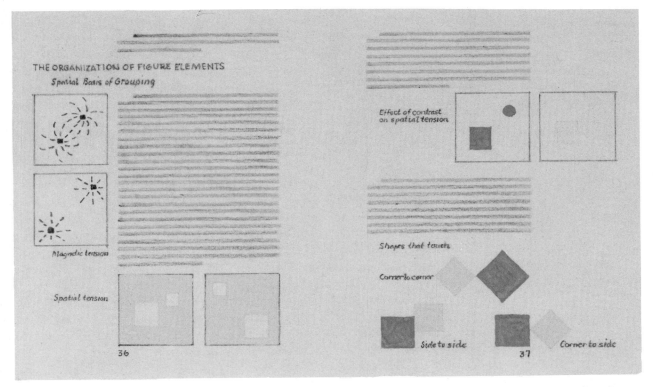

Double-page spread in the presentation dummy

tempt to finish these with the precision that would be necessary for reproduction, but they had to be sufficiently accurate in tone and carefully enough executed to demonstrate their point.

Finally, text and illustrations were complete except for this chapter, which could not be written until the book was accepted and the proposed layout criticized. When I placed it with McGraw-Hill, they not only accepted the manuscript, but were kind enough to let me do the layout for the book as well.

PRODUCTION

A great many problems arose to modify the form of the book as presented in the full-scale dummy. Some of these had to do with expression and style. Most of them concerned the technical problems of reproduction and economics. I shall not attempt to give a blow-by-blow account of all the adjustments and revisions. It will serve our purpose as well to consider two representative cases, one primarily a technical matter, the other economic.

The first concerned the selection of a type face for the body of the text. The publisher's production department felt that Scotch Modern was a poor choice for offset reproduction. The difficulty is is that this face is characterized by strong contrast between the heavy strokes and the hairlines. In order not to lose the hairlines, the plate is apt to be overexposed in the photographic process. This causes the heavy strokes to thicken, making the text too black. From their fund of experience, they concluded that a lighter face with slightly heavier hairlines would give a better balanced and more distinguished effect. Monotype Baskerville No. 353 was therefore substituted for my original selection. They also advised the substitution of eleven-point type with two points of leading in place of my twelve-point on fourteen. They felt this was more in keeping with the textbook nature of the work.

This change meant that the copy fitting, and consequently the whole layout, had to be thoroughly revised. It was unnecessary to carry this out in the same detail as the presentation dummy. An accurate indication of copy and the size and placement of illustrations sufficed.

The second problem had to do with color reproductions. In the original layout, color occurred on thirty-eight pages in six signatures. This would have meant at least thirty-six press runs and thirty-eight separate color plates to prepare. The cost of this plan would have made the sales price of the book too high to fit the text use for which it is intended. I quite appreciated the necessity for a more economical solution. At the same time, I was very reluctant to sacrifice the principle of co-ordinating the text and illustrations by grouping all the color. That obviously was the most economical solution.

Consequently, in revising the layout, I tried to find a new organization for the color material that would be in better proportion to cost. I reconsidered all my illustrations. In a few cases, I substituted

190

directions for you, as readers, to execute things I had originally illustrated. (The methods of controlling value are a case in point.) Most of the trouble came in the color chapters. These had occupied three signatures with color on both sides of the sheet. That meant at least twenty-four runs through the press. I tried to get the material into two signatures with illustrations on one side only.

After exploring the alternative organizations for several days, I reached the conclusion that any solution that was reasonably practical from the production angle, would mean the elimination of essential illustrations. Reluctantly, I took up the alternative grouping all the color in a number of plates.

Once this decision was made, I discovered the law of compensation applied. Although I lost that intimate co-ordination between text and illustration which I felt to be one of the distinctions of the rest of the book, the visual co-ordination between the color illustrations themselves was more effective. For example: originally, the structure of hue intervals had to be separated by twenty-four pages from the application of those intervals. The new plan permitted grouping these related ideas in one plate. (See Plate II.)

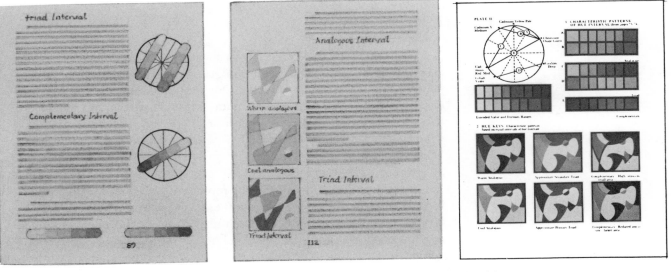

Original layout plan.   Revision.

The final result was that only three of the original illustrations were omitted, two because I considered the description sufficiently clear in itself (control of value, for instance), and the other because the degree of accuracy necessary to prove the point would have been too expensive (sixteen tones of green, see page 70). Instead of six signatures containing color and thirty-six runs through the press, the seven color plates occur on one side of signature seven, requir-

191

ing four runs. Something of value is sacrificed, but for a greater value. The price of the book is brought into a reasonable range without seriously compromising its quality.

This sort of limitation is met in many design problems. The solution, in this case, is a compromise only in the sense that my lack of experience led me into visualizing an impractical form. If I had known more about book production, I would have realized this and accepted the limitation from the start. This is another way of saying that my understanding of material and technique was incomplete and led, as always, to an unsatisfactory formal concept.

One related point: The publisher's production department was most helpful in suggesting changes where the selection of other tones would make the reproduction simpler. In many of the diagrams, my point could be demonstrated with equal effectiveness in a different palette of tones. In some cases my original choice presented special difficulties. The wide technical experience they could bring to bear on the problem was an invaluable guide in ironing out unnecessary difficulties of this sort.

CONCLUSION

I hope this tour backstage, so to speak, has been interesting. To those readers whose field lies in typography and layout, it may have contributed information of value. Our real purpose, though, had to do with these techniques only incidentally. It was rather because the book presents a concrete design problem and its solution which the reader and I can share that we have discussed it at length. Here we have the design process in action from the first formulation of purpose to the final solution.

I have tried to illustrate and emphasize the relationships and interdependencies of the four causal essentials, the purpose, and the formal, the material, and the technical causes. The parallel connection of formal and structural relations has also been concretely demonstrated. We have, of necessity, had to consider these problems in one limited frame of reference. The details of the process will be different for every problem you undertake. Its spirit, its organic unity is always the same.

We have had to approach this unity analytically in order to discuss it fruitfully and coherently. You are probably aware, though, that the analytical distinctions are sharper in the Introduction, where we are generalizing, than in this chapter. When we are designing, we do not stop to ask, "Is this a technical cause or a material cause?" As our creative potential becomes trained, as we gain experience with our materials and techniques, the unity of

192

designing is indeed organic. It is so much a unity that no element can really be segregated without doing violence both to it and to the process as a whole. It is the same with any organic unity. The dissected heart is not the real organ functioning in its appointed way in our human metabolism. Still, dissection is necessary as a basis for understanding the living heart. Analysis is our only means for getting at the complex of factors on which our design judgments are made. Even in this chapter, where we have tried to treat the synthesis, we can only picture it, not recreate it. Nothing can do that except your own creative experience. I hope this book may help you to enrich and mature that experience through a better understanding of its structure and a more critical awareness of all that is involved.

INDEX